LESTER
RETURN OF A LEGEND

JOHN KARTER

HEADLINE

First published in 1992
by HEADLINE BOOK PUBLISHING PLC

First published in paperback in 1993
by HEADLINE BOOK PUBLISHING PLC

10 9 8 7 6 5 4 3 2 1

ISBN 0 7472 7922 5

Typeset by Columns Design & Production Services Ltd, Reading

Colour illustration reproduction by Koford, Singapore

Printed and bound in Great Britain by
BPCC Hazells Ltd, Member of BPCC Ltd.

HEADLINE BOOK PUBLISHING PLC
Headline House
79 Great Titchfield Street
London W1P 7FN

CONTENTS

ACKNOWLEDGEMENTS

Racing is often a closed world, but the mere mention of Lester's name was a key to opening many doors. Racing folk were only too happy to talk about Lester and in this respect I am eternally grateful to the following in particular: Robert Armstrong, Sandy Barclay, Mark Beecroft, Clive Brittain, Michael Caulfield, Henry Cecil, Julie Cecil, Bryn Crossley, John Gosden, Michael Hinchliffe, Darryl Holland, Fulke Johnson Houghton, Geoff Lewis, Jimmy Lindley, Joe Mercer, Alan Munro, Vincent O'Brien, Jacqueline O'Brien, Bruce Raymond, Charles St George, Robert Sangster, Michael Stoute, Michael Watt and Geoff Wragg.

I would also like to thank Michael Harris of the *Racing Post* and Lawrie Kelsey of the *Cambridge Evening News* for allowing me access to their files.

PREFACE

I was first introduced to the peerless talents of Lester Piggott as a fifteen-year-old schoolboy when my grandfather took me to Epsom for my initiation into the hypnotically colourful world of the Turf. I knew absolutely nothing about horse racing and even less about the subtleties of race riding, but watching Lester cruising home on the favourite in the last race had me spellbound. From that moment on I was hooked, not just on racing but on the perennial genius of this extraordinary man.

How did he do it, I asked myself after he had spirited his mount from last to first, in less time than it takes to tear up a betting ticket, without appearing actually to *do* anything. The crowds were ecstatic, and it was patently clear that they were not merely reacting through their pockets.

To the cheering masses Lester was a folk hero, a figure held in unique public affection and esteem, arguably more famed and feted in his way than other sporting greats like Stanley Matthews or Len Hutton. Like millions of others I came to regard Lester as inimitable and irreplaceable, and I consider myself fortunate to have witnessed him performing his special brand of magic at first hand.

Much has been made of Lester's allegedly less attractive traits – far too much, in my opinion. We must never forget that underneath the legend he is just an ordinary man. He has human weaknesses, but in that respect who is to say that he is any worse than the rest of us? And in the one case where his foolishness brought about his downfall at the hands of the authorities, he was made to pay heavily for his folly.

I have therefore deliberately not sought to dwell on the controversial aspects of Lester's life, bringing them in only where necessary as part of the overall picture. Lester has brought so much pleasure to millions and it is this positive element that I hope comes through above all in what is intended essentially as a tribute to a remarkable character.

I jumped at the chance to write this book because Lester has fired my imagination beyond any other racing personality. Perhaps the most fascinating aspect of my research was that in talking to so many people who knew Lester professionally and personally I genuinely did not encounter one person who had anything really bad to say about the man. Most spoke of him with deep affection and respect and all were unanimous in placing his extraordinary talent on a plane of its own.

FOR MY SONS, BEN AND RYAN

CHAPTER ONE
THE SEEDS OF GREATNESS

Joe Mercer, craggy-faced veteran of a thousand racetrack battles, sat back in his armchair in the low-beamed sitting room of his Berkshire farmhouse with tears rolling down his cheek.

On the television screen in front of Mercer a face almost as familiar as the one that greeted him in the mirror each morning beamed out at him from the heady mayhem of Belmont Park racecourse in New York. Surrounded by a frenzied mob of media men, Lester Piggott, Mercer's lifelong friend and former arch-rival, was talking a spellbound global audience through a sporting miracle that had taken place moments earlier. If Mercer felt at all ridiculous about blubbering like a baby he had no reason to do so. Millions of misty-eyed onlookers had been swept along on an extraordinary flood tide of emotion as Piggott, just nine days short of his fifty-fifth birthday, rolled back the years and galloped away with the million-dollar Breeders' Cup Mile on Royal Academy.

The euphoria gripped professionals and public alike. Trainers, owners and hard-bitten horse players, to whom Piggott was quite simply the best jockey there had ever been, fought self-consciously against lumps in their throats, wondering if they were going soft in their old age. Betting-shop regulars who backed Lester blind every day of the week and once-a-year dabblers who had risked their 50 pences religiously on him in the Derby, convinced that he and only he had a divine right to win it, rubbed disbelieving eyes and said a silent prayer of thanks.

Many must have asked themselves whether it was all just a dream. A few days previously the man had been history, consigned irretrievably to racing's pantheon after five years languishing in the depressing shadows of retirement. The impossible deeds in the saddle that he had carried out daily were just magnificent memories.

When Piggott jumped down from the back of Wind From The West at Nottingham almost five years previously and turned his back on a career that had patently not run its course, his departure left a black hole in the racing scene that no man, not even champions of the calibre of Pat Eddery, Steve Cauthen and Willie Carson, could ever hope to fill. On the day Lester hung up his riding boots,

Phil Bull, the creator of racing's 'bible', *Timeform*, summed up Piggott's unique professional standing admirably.

'There were many fine jockeys riding in my youth, Steve Donoghue, Joe Childs, Charlie Elliott and others, even before the days of Gordon Richards and Harry Wragg,' Bull said. 'But for me Lester is the greatest. He excels in his understanding of not only the horses he rides but those he is riding against. That's what makes him the supreme tactician.'

Yet Bull's tribute was wholly inadequate in explaining the phenomenon that was Lester. It is doubtful if any name has conjured up such myth and magic. He was man and superman; hero and villain; a flawed genius with a gift from the angels. He inspired a billion bets and also a thousand stories, some true but most apocryphal, distorting his personality to monstrous proportions. For those who prefer their heroes with a sprinkling of wickedness, Piggott certainly fitted the bill, becoming racing's most controversial figure in a way not dissimilar to, say, George Best or John McEnroe in their respective sports. He earned a reputation as a hard man and a loner, pursuing his own relentless course with a 'two fingers to the world' attitude. Those famous ravaged features, as cracked and dry as the prairie in a drought, revealed nothing of his emotions. Loping into the paddock, whip clutched by his side like a loaded gun, he put you in mind of Clint Eastwood in a spaghetti western. His enormous presence allied to his bad-boy image and his uncanny magic on horseback imbued him with a film-star quality and for this reason he transcended the world of horse racing like no other.

On 29 October 1985 the legend had been lost for ever – or so it seemed until Piggott stunned the world with an impromptu comeback the week before the Breeders' Cup. While racing folk hailed his return, however, there was also widespread scepticism as to his ability to re-create the old magic, and a handful of winners in the days leading up to Belmont had seemed unconvincing evidence of his resurrection. But now, as the satellite beamed those vivid pictures of the Breeders' Cup spectacular across the water there was no room left for doubt. Lester was back, not merely in name, not just a pale shadow of his former greatness, but in all his glory. The spine-tingling triumph of Royal Academy had proved that beyond all question.

In the seething amphitheatre of Belmont in front of more than 50,000 baying fans, Piggott had produced a virtuoso performance that equalled any of the fabulous feats of race riding that had entranced the crowds during thirty-seven years in the saddle. With that immaculate sense of timing and the almost demonic will to win that had gained him eleven jockeys' championships and over 5,000 winners worldwide, Piggott had brought Royal Academy charging through from last to first, thrusting the colt's head in front in the shadow of the winning post with the aid of one of those famous 'rat-tat-tat' finishes from his whip. Then, basking in the afterglow of what was arguably his most remarkable victory – certainly his most valuable – he informed us in typically laconic Piggott fashion

Piggott's good friend and colleague, Joe Mercer, displays his OBE after his investiture at Buckingham Palace in 1980. Piggott received his OBE five years earlier, but was stripped of the award in 1988

that it had been as easy as sitting on a rocking horse.

As Mercer watched Brough Scott, the Channel Four presenter, take Lester through a re-run of that impossible American dream he was deeply moved but not overly surprised by what he was seeing. Joe and Lester had retired within days of each other five years earlier – Lester had said 'I'll give up when you give up' – and Joe had kept in constant touch with his old sparring partner, visiting him twice in gaol when Piggott was serving his year inside for tax offences. Himself a former champion jockey and now enjoying a new role as racing manager to Sheikh Maktoum Al Maktoum, the ruler of Dubai, Mercer was therefore as well placed as anyone outside Piggott's immediate family to know what moves the maestro might make and, more to the point, what he was capable of achieving.

'Lester is Lester. He's a man you never doubt. How could I be surprised by anything he does?' Mercer says. 'He has always kept himself incredibly fit and he had been riding out two lots a day for his wife Susan at their Newmarket yard, so it didn't really amaze me to see him pull his boots on again, nor to see him come back to the top so quickly.'

Yet, even knowing his old friend the way he did, Mercer was still utterly poleaxed by the piece of Piggott theatre that had been acted out so dramatically round that lush strip of turf on Long Island. Like others who had got close to Piggott – as close, that is, as this enigmatic man would ever let anyone get – and managed to break through the wall of myth that surrounded him, Mercer had nothing but the utmost respect for Piggott, both as a professional and a man. To see Lester spring back from the twilight zone of an unfulfilling retirement gladdened Joe's heart with the sort of warm glow that he had experienced only once before. 'There have been two fairy stories in my life,' Mercer says. 'The first was Bob Champion fighting back from cancer to win the Grand National on Aldaniti. The second was Lester Piggott turning back the years to win the Breeders' Cup on Royal Academy.'

Mercer had plenty of company as Piggott's cup overflowed. It is a fair bet that Saturday 27 October 1990 was the day when millions of grown men started to believe in fairy tales.

Iris Piggott must have felt a similar kind of trembling emotion as she glanced down at the small pink bundle she lay holding in the delivery room of Wantage Hospital in Berkshire on the night of 5 November 1935.

If Iris allowed herself to daydream as she reflected on the birth of her first and only child it can only have been in one direction. As little Lester Keith howled his disapproval at the outside world, there would have been no idle thoughts of him becoming a great lawyer, surgeon or politician. Virtually as soon as Lester's rattle and bootees were discarded they would be replaced by a racing whip and riding boots. The future for Iris's lusty lad was already engraved in stone.

More literally, it was to be engraved in elegant black lettering on a special Lester Piggott panel in the National Horseracing Museum, situated in the heartland of British racing in Newmarket High Street. The museum contains some fascinating items of Piggott memorabilia and in a quiet corner of Gallery Four visitors can read a summary of Lester's forebears and peruse the Piggott family tree which reveals that his racing pedigree, stretching back over 200 years, is virtually as long as those of the great horses he has ridden.

Piggott's family had been involved in horse racing for six generations. On his father's side he traces back to an intriguing eighteenth-century character called John Day, a Hampshire trainer and associate of the Prince of Wales. Day and his sons were as renowned for their nefarious deeds on the Turf as they were for their many great successes. Lester's paternal grandfather, Ernie Piggott, won the Grand National three times and was thrice champion National Hunt jockey. Lester's great-uncle, Mornington Cannon, was champion Flat jockey six times and won six Classics, while another great-uncle, Kempton Cannon, rode three Classic winners. His father, Keith, was a leading jump jockey and champion National Hunt trainer, sending out Ayala to win the 1963 Grand National at 66–1.

Piggott's mother, Iris, herself a fine rider and twice winner of the historic Newmarket Town Plate for amateurs, was a member of another great racing family, the Rickabys. Her great-grandfather, Fred Rickaby, trained a Derby winner and three other relatives rode to eleven Classic successes between them. Her father, also named Fred, claimed three; her brother, Frederick Lester Rickaby, notched up five; and her nephew, Bill, took three in a career spanning four decades, two of which were frequently spent chasing the disappearing backside of an infuriatingly talented cousin named Lester Piggott.

The racing family Piggott: Lester, aged sixteen, with his father, Keith, and mother, Iris, at their home in Lambourn

Yet even though the shape of Lester's life had been determined centuries previously, Iris could have had no inkling of the unique status her new-born son would achieve. She would have been justified in expecting him to make his mark in the racing world, certainly. But how could she possibly have known that the infant in her arms was to become an international hero, a man whose face would stare out at the world from newspapers, magazines and television screens almost daily, as instantly recognisable as a prime minister or a pop star.

Whether you believe in such things or not, perhaps some hint of the young Piggott's destiny lay in the stars. The 'science' of astrology is still treated with widespread scepticism, yet while most of us accept that those horoscopes we scan so eagerly every day are by and large nonsensical trivia, there is often a remarkable degree of accuracy in the personality profiles laid down by our star signs. Piggott was born under Scorpio, the sign of the scorpion, among whose more illustrious subjects are Mrs Indira Gandhi, Viscount Montgomery, Princess Grace of Monaco, Billy Graham and Field Marshal Erwin Rommel. The following brief extracts from a leading reference work on astrology describe some of the traits of the Scopio personality.

Still waters run deep is perhaps a good way to summarise Scorpio's mental attitude. His most overwhelming characteristics are his intensity and sense of purpose. He cannot skim the surface, whether he is preparing for a university degree or simply reading the Sunday newspapers; the pitch of intensity at which he must live simply will not allow it.

The Scorpio will work extremely hard to achieve his ambitions – then quite suddenly will abandon everything and start again from nothing. He has an enormously high energy level and is rather like a powerful engine which will deteriorate if left idle. If he finds he is involved in work which seems to him to be unimportant, or if he feels he is simply a small cog in a large wheel he won't function properly. He responds to discipline, but it is the discipline of action and energy expended, not the discipline of restriction, confinement or repression. (From *The Compleat Astrologer's Sun-Signs Guide* by Derek and Julia Parker.)

It cannot be disputed that those few statements provide a recognisable if rough sketch of Piggott the man and the professional. Indeed, with regard to at least one major area of his life, it is remarkably prophetic, as we shall see later.

Returning to a more conventional guideline, that of pedigree, one thing is for sure. If the young Lester Keith Piggott had been a racehorse his bloodlines would have had the cognoscenti turning up at the sales in droves, eager to snap up a youngster whose genes bore the finest designer labels.

Looking at this thoroughbred infant, however, no one, not even his parents, could have realised that nature had saddled Lester with two significant handicaps. Indeed, he was anything but custom-built to make a top-flight jockey, primarily because his mature height of 5ft 7½in would make him a relative giant in a Lilliputian world. As far as making progress towards Flat racing's summit was concerned, Piggott's size would eventually dictate two significant adaptations to nature. First, because he could not mould his frame into the conventional jockey's crouch, he was forced to develop a unique style. It was a style that at first sight looked absurd and awkward, and was absolute anathema to the purist, yet it worked far more effectively than any traditional textbook method. Mark Beecroft, senior race-riding instructor at the British School of Racing, summarises Piggott's technique in the following way.

'Piggott was not a natural jockey. Because he was so tall he had to adapt his style and he developed a unique way of riding that all the youngsters tried to copy but none could master.

'He raised his knees to six inches above the withers and transferred his weight on to the front of the horse. He didn't use his heels to drive his mounts, but had fantastic balance and relied on his incredible strength and fitness, and his whip.'

Perched high over his mount with his bottom thrust absurdly high in the air, it was easy to pick Piggott out even in a huge field of runners. Clad in gaudy silks he

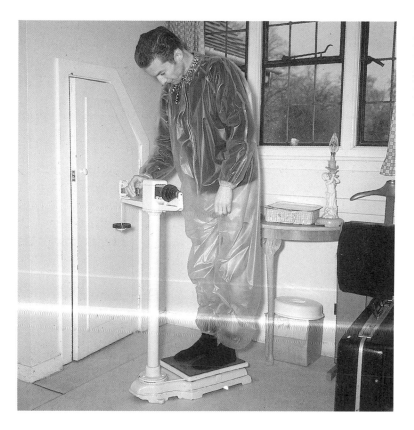

Sweating it out: Piggott, seen here encased in his 'torture suit', had to maintain the most spartan regime to keep his body at some two stone below his natural body weight

resembled one of those exotic African birds that cheekily hitch a ride on a hippo's back. When someone once asked him why he put his bottom in the air like that he came out with the now famous reply: 'Well, I've got to put it somewhere!'

Piggott said on his retirement: 'Young jockeys would do well to copy Joe Mercer rather than me. If they copy me they might break their necks.' He almost did that himself several times during a career peppered with bone-crunching falls and agonising injuries, many of them due at least in part to a style that might have looked more at home in a circus.

Piggott once pointed out that his above-average size gave him a vital edge in strength when it came to driving home a horse in a tight finish. Its biggest disadvantage, by far, was the need to keep his body weight down to about two stone below its natural level, an extraordinary feat of self-denial that was reflected in that gaunt, heavily etched face. Other jockeys have continually expressed their amazement at Piggott's ability to exist on what was once described as a diet of fresh air, the *Sporting Life* and a fat cigar. It seemed impossible that he could eat like a sparrow and then lift horses over the finishing line with the strength of an Arnold Schwarzenegger. There was some talk of his father persuading him to use powerful wasting drugs to keep his weight down in the early days and that may well have been true. In his autobiography *Life in the Saddle*, the great Russian jockey Nikolai Nasibov recalls a memory of Lester in the weighing room when they were riding against each other in Paris.

'To the left I saw Lester Piggott. Yes, that Lester's got real jockeys' blood. But where's he got his height from? Such a strapping lad from a family of jockeys! How does he make the weight? Must live on laxatives and emetics!'

Many others have given up the unequal struggle, notably the great nineteenth-century rider, Fred Archer, who shot himself when the cumulative effects of years of bodily abuse unbalanced his mind. For Piggott, though, unwavering self-denial simply became a way of life. He had no choice, being only too aware that to ride at anything much above 8st 6lb would let in lighter rivals, and his insatiable quest for winners overcame everything, including the most dreadful hunger pangs. Contrary to popular belief, however, Piggott did eat some meals, albeit in tiny, bird-like quantities. And when it came to chocolates and ice cream he could be a positive glutton.

Size also mattered to Lester from the psychological point of view. Jimmy Lindley, once a leading rival and now a BBC commentator, says: 'Lester had a complex about being taller than the other jockeys, particularly as it made him stand out when he walked into the parade ring. I think he would have liked to be five or six inches shorter and I also think that was one of the reasons why he rode so short.'

There was another problem apart from his size that marked Lester down as anything but the perfect specimen. When he was still only about five it was discovered that he was substantially deaf. This defect diminished over the years, but it became a feature of his character and gave rise to a whole host of Lester jokes, such as the old favourite about the stable boy who asked him tentatively: 'How about a quid for that winner I did you [was in charge of], Lester?' Piggott replied: 'I can't hear you, that's my bad ear.' The stable boy went round to his other side and said: 'What about a couple of quid for that winner I did for you?' Lester: 'I still can't hear you. Try the one pound ear again.' Lester certainly used his deafness to his advantage, as Nasibov recalls. 'He's quite a gentleman really, but you've got to watch it with him when he's racing. He once crossed me; rode right across my nose. "What do you think you're playing at?" I asked him in the paddock afterwards. "I'm sorry, sir," he said. "I'm a little deaf and I didn't hear your hooves."'

Piggott could lip-read fluently and one advantage of his deafness was that he could pretend not to hear irritating questions, shutting himself off from the incessant pressures of fame that subjected him to what he once described as a goldfish-bowl existence. His hearing problem, together with a resultant speech impediment, was undoubtedly a contributory factor in making him withdrawn and uncommunicative, but it was by no means the sole reason. Piggott was one of those rare people who are quite happy in their own company and do not need validation from others. Why bother wasting words with parasitic hangers-on – so

Sweeping to victory: Life was not all glamour for the young Lester, seen here as a twelve-year-old mucking out at his father's Lambourn stables

many of the people he came into contact with were no more – when he could be getting on with what he did best? Horses were far less trouble and far more lucrative than people. Lester once revealed a little of that inner self when he said: 'I have often read that I'm good and so dedicated to make up for my deafness. That's a load of tripe in my book. People who do things well and become famous are always said to do so to compensate for something like an unhappy childhood or their mother being shot or something. The reason I am where I am is because I work extremely hard and I love riding and the thrill of it all.'

So there was the young Lester, exquisitely bred for the job, but by no means born with the ideal equipment for it. Nevertheless, a jockey he was going to be – Keith had probably decided that long before Lester made his entrance into the world – and nothing could alter that chosen course. Lester was indeed riding almost before he could walk. He cut his equestrian teeth on a spirited pony named Brandy, enjoyed great success at local gymkhanas and was riding out racehorses at his father's small Berkshire yard before his tenth birthday. Piggott senior moved to a bigger establishment in Lambourn when his son was eleven and in 1948, at the age of twelve, Lester became officially apprenticed to him as a jockey.

At that time Lester had moved from the parish school of King Alfred's at Wantage and was attending a small private school in Upper Lambourn some two or three miles away from his father's yard. He would ride work on the horses in the morning before making his way miserably on his bike to the daily academic grind. School held about as much interest for him as an afternoon at the local morgue. Thoughts of riding sleek Thoroughbreds to victory in front of delirious crowds were the only thing that set young Lester's blood racing and the way he acted out his fantasy gave an early indication of his all-consuming will to win. As Lester cycled along the leafy Berkshire lanes he would imagine himself surging up the finishing straight at Newmarket or Epsom. Jimmy Lindley explains: 'Lester would ride his bike and imagine he was in a race. He would ride finishes using a stick as his whip and trees and telegraph poles as winning posts. One day another kid got in front of him and Lester was so incensed that he stuck his stick through the other kid's wheel.'

The real thing came at Haydock Park on a blustery Wednesday in August 1948 when Lester was just twelve years old. Riding a three-year-old filly named The Chase, on whom he had made his public debut at Salisbury five months earlier, Piggott scuttled home ahead of Davy Jones on Prompt Corner to chalk up the first of those five thousand plus winners. Jones, on the runner-up, was apparently none too bothered about winning and Lester, weighing under five stone, his over-large jockey's cap accentuating his cherubic face, looked as if he might have been more at home singing in a boys' choir than booting home half a ton of skittish horseflesh. Never mind. The most celebrated career in racing was off the mark. Lester Piggott the jockey had arrived.

His mother told the press: 'He's just an ordinary boy. Don't make a fuss of

RIGHT Young Stoneface: The chubby cheeks of fourteen-year-old Lester present a marked contrast to his ravaged look in later life. Even then, however, the stern-faced determination showed

BELOW Charlie Smirke on Tulyar looks back at Piggott on Gay Time as they pass the post in the 1952 Derby. Piggott blamed himself for losing the race after being out manoeuvred by Smirke

him.' But they did; yet as is so often the way of things there was a sobering hiatus thereafter which left Lester waiting over a year for his second success and brought him only six winners during the following season. This was, however, merely one of a handful of inconsequential blips on the progress chart. During the 1950 season Lester rode the socks off the other lads and cantered away with the title of champion apprentice with a score of fifty-two. He was still just a scrawny fourteen-year-old with a shiny face and an unbroken voice, but every time the established names of the weighing room pulled on their riding boots they knew they had the hungry shadow of a boy genius riding up behind them.

Lester was again leading apprentice in 1951, a significant year in his burgeoning career despite the fact that he broke his leg and missed the final quarter of the season. A first major-league success on the French horse, Mystery IX, in the Eclipse Stakes at Sandown Park was the pearl, and a flawed jewel named Zucchero carried him on to the world stage for a debut role in a part that he was to stamp with his own unique artistry, for this dark and brooding colt became Lester's first ride in the Derby. However, while this race was responsible above all else for making him a national idol, his opening shot aboard a brilliant but quirky animal was not a memorable one. Piggott's persuasiveness was to make him the only man capable of out-psyching Zucchero – the following year they won the Coronation Cup over the Derby course – but on this occasion he failed to do so. The horse's refusal to take part in the race until far too late relieved Lester of any blame, but his perfectionist mentality doubtless caused him to brood on the debacle for some time.

Piggott certainly blamed himself for the defeat of Gay Time a year later. That second Derby ride might have looked an exemplary one, but Piggott felt he had been outwitted by the wily old fox Charlie Smirke on Tulyar. He was not so much outwitted as the victim of what footballers term a professional foul: Smirke, having taken the lead some way from home, allowed his mount to swerve across Lester and impede him as he made his challenge. To compound the agony Gay Time threw Piggott heavily shortly after they passed the post. Gay Time bolted, so Piggott was too late to object, but the owner would not countenance such an unsporting move anyway.

Piggott reflected later that if he had not been so raw and inexperienced the cocky Smirke would never have made his famous 'What did I Tulyar?' remark as he dismounted. 'Lots of things went wrong. We were slowly away and Gay Time lost a shoe beforehand,' Piggott said. 'But basically I didn't ride the right race on him and I never forgave myself for losing that Derby. When Gay Time threw me it was probably his way of telling me that I rode a stinker.'

Some stinker. Many older jockeys never showed the instinctive mastery of Epsom's notorious switchback that the sixteen-year-old Piggott had demonstrated on Gay Time. He erased the memory of Smirkie's smirk two years later, but before then the going suddenly became unexpectedly hard for young Lester.

Bottoms up: Lester's famous posterior is even higher than usual as he survives a jumping error by Prince Charlemagne to win the Triumph Hurdle at Hurst Park during a brief but highly successful spell over hurdles

Indeed, it looked at one point as if the kid with the world of Flat racing at his feet might walk out of the game altogether.

At the age of seventeen Piggott was something of a gangling mess in professional terms. His weight soared and he found winners elusive, the lack of success bringing with it a crisis of confidence that would not be the last in his career. A switch to the heavier world of jump racing seemed logical, particularly as his father had been so successful in that sphere. During the 1953–4 National Hunt season Piggott's famous bottom was to be spotted even higher in the air as he soared round the hurdles circuit with conspicuous aplomb. His acute sense of balance made him a natural and he netted nine wins from twenty-five rides, including the prestigious Triumph Hurdle on Prince Charlemagne. Nine more successes came his way in a lingering flirtation with jumping over the next few years, but thankfully he had already made a renewed commitment to the Flat

Piggott cruises to a first Derby triumph on Never Say Die in 1954. Afterwards, he annoyed reporters by describing his victory as 'just another race'

after that first winter of discontent. And glorious summer returned to his career in the shape of a surprise package, propitiously named Never Say Die.

Odds of 33–1 about a Lester Piggott Derby runner might sound unbelievable now, but on that first Wednesday in June 1954 the public did not see it that way. They knew eighteen-year-old Piggott was a bit special, but could not possibly foresee the magical Epsom odyssey he was about to embark on, using his unique gift to hone the complex problems of riding in the Derby to a fine art. And even if they had accepted, as the great Irish trainer Vincent O'Brien once said, that Piggott was 7lb better than any other jockey at Epsom, the sketchy form of Never Say Die, who had gained one win from nine starts, would hardly have inspired

26

confidence. The colt's veteran trainer, Joe Lawson, did not find jockeys falling over themselves to take the mount and he had worked some way down his list before he sent Lester a telegram ten days before the race offering him the ride.

Looking at those grainy old black-and-white newsreels of Never Say Die's triumph, the film flickering around like a home movie, it is not at all easy to follow the action. One thing that stands out unmistakably, however, is the calm authority of Piggott's riding. It would have been impressive for a man with twice his experience, but for an eighteen-year-old taking on twenty-one rivals in the maelstrom of Epsom it was quite remarkable. No rider can do the job without the right horse, of course, but the way Piggott steered his course round the world's most demanding racetrack was eerie. Even in that first victory his path seemed almost pre-ordained as he stalked the leaders rounding Tattenham Corner and then cut them down with a style and economy of effort that could only be marvelled at.

With Derby number one in the bag, Piggott showed the world the merest hint of a smile as he rode into the hallowed winner's circle. Then he infuriated the gaggle of pressmen who pounced on him like marauding hawks by shrugging it all off with his famous phrase, 'It was just another race.'

Soon afterwards his father whisked him back to Lambourn in the family Alvis and Lester was tucked up in bed by nine o'clock. That was the way Keith wanted it for his son – no fuss, no frills and therefore, he hoped, no spoiling or squandering of the precocious talent. Lester slept contentedly that night, but he would not have done had he known what was in store for him just a fortnight later.

By the time of the 1954 Derby the young Piggott had earned himself a reputation for something else besides outstanding ability in the saddle. Nine suspensions, the bulk of them for careless riding, appeared to indicate that he was a hot-headed young man who, in his hunger for success, would bulldoze his rivals aside without a backward glance. The truth was substantially different, even though Lester, it must be said, was frequently out of line. Geoff Lewis, one of his old rivals and now a successful trainer at Epsom, puts it this way: 'At that time Lester was a bit of a desperado. He would go for gaps that weren't there and wouldn't let anything get in his way.' What Piggott did, however, was no worse than what many young sportsmen in a hurry to reach the top do – he bent the rules a little. Several previous champions in racing have been just as audacious in their youth, notably the nine times title-holder Pat Eddery, nicknamed Polyfilla by the other jockeys because of his inclination to fill up the narrowest of gaps.

Part of the blame for Piggott's attitude could be put down to his father, who had been known as a wickedly hard man in the saddle – he once deliberately sent an amateur rival crashing through the wings of a fence and joked 'Just keeping in practice.' Piggott senior had drummed into his son that it was not the done thing to be a wimp and that he should never let anyone get the better of him. Go for

Another double century for the great Sir Gordon Richards as he brings home a winner at Lingfield Park. Gordon saw Lester as a threat, but although the rivalry between them was fierce Richards later dispelled rumours of serious animosity by offering Piggott the job as his stable jockey when he began training

broke and bugger the rest of them seemed to be the philosophy instilled in Piggott junior. So Lester took his chances when he could, but he was certainly not psychotic or in any way dangerous. Nevertheless, that was how the stewards viewed him and it is obvious that the presiding panel of officials at Royal Ascot were prejudiced beyond redemption when Piggott was hauled before them to explain his part in a controversial finish to the *King Edward VII Stakes* two weeks after the 1954 Derby.

The action is always fast and frenetic in the short Ascot straight as the runners wheel round the bend like motorcyclists, jostling furiously for position. Even by the usual standards, however, this King Edward was something of a hot potato, and Lester, who was again aboard Never Say Die, encountered more trouble than he could have imagined in his worst nightmares as he lunged for a gap on the inside. At that point familiar shouts of 'Come on, Gordon' announced the arrival on the scene of Sir Gordon Richards. Everyone's favourite, Gordon had dominated the Flat racing scene since winning the first of his twenty-six jockeys' championships in 1927. Now, riding Rashleigh, he made his move on the outside at almost precisely the same time as Piggott. In between them, Lester's cousin, Bill Rickaby on Garter, became the meat in a sandwich as both Never Say Die and Rashleigh veered off a true line under pressure. Others were getting into a tangle, too, and the race developed into a rugby scrum.

The stewards initially lodged an objection to Rashleigh, who finished first, but there was no camera patrol film to assist them in those days and they had to rely on their own eyes and the evidence of the jockeys. Gordon said that Lester had barged his way out, but Lester, who finished fourth on Never Say Die, claimed that Gordon had deliberately pushed Garter across on to him to block his path. In the war of words with the elder statesman of the jockeys, Lester never stood a chance; it was justice of the roughest kind. He was suspended for the remainder of the meeting and reported to the Stewards of the Jockey Club, racing's ruling body. Two weeks later came the announcement that turned Lester's cosy world upside down. In a judgement of unprecedented ferocity, the stewards said that they had '. . . taken notice of his dangerous and erratic riding both this season and in previous seasons and that in spite of continuous warnings he continued to show complete disregard for the rules and the safety of other jockeys'. They withdrew his jockey's licence and stated that he would not be allowed to re-apply for it until he had spent six months away from his father at another training establishment.

Piggott has since described the stewards as 'old fuddy duddies' and claimed, quite rightly, that during the later part of his career the offence would have brought him a seven-day suspension at most. Piggott has always hated pomposity, and the stiff-upper-lipped military types who ran British racing were anathema to him. For their part, the stewards regarded Piggott as a little upstart, an irritating mosquito who had to be squashed. Jimmy Lindley sheds further light, alluding to Piggott's distinct lack of communication skills. 'Lester was not the greatest talker and he found it difficult to explain himself. He also didn't really understand what the stewards were getting at. He appeared arrogant and Gordon did him no favours.'

When the evidence is looked at dispassionately, it seems clear that Piggott was only marginally in the wrong and that Richards was the villain of the piece both in the stewards' room and the race itself. Geoff Lewis, who rode in the Ascot event, says: 'Lester was going for a legitimate gap, but Gordon and the older jockeys were getting tired of his recklessness and if the opportunity arose to shut the door in his face they would do so. That was what happened at Ascot.'

The annoyance of the senior jockeys is easy to understand, but it seems there

Piggott with Geoff Lewis, who despite their great rivalry has always been one of Lester's most ardent admirers

was a darker side to all this. The Never Say Die affair came towards the end of a period known as the golden age of jockeyship when men like Richards, Smirke, Charlie Elliott, Harry Wragg and Doug Smith thrilled the crowds with their skills. But this adulation masked the fact that those famous names were also hard men who, unfettered by the camera patrol, sometimes used crude tactics rather than finesse to facilitate their passage. Young boys, particularly those with a precocious talent like Lester, were regarded as nuisances to be slapped down whenever possible. Jimmy Lindley explains: 'Lester had to be reckless because there was so much more cut and thrust then and the older jockeys were out to get him.'

In Gordon's case this harshness may well have been somewhat personal. That is not to say that there was any real animosity, but Richards recognised that Piggott was the heir apparent to his crown and he did not want to abdicate before he was ready. Who could blame him for looking anxiously over his shoulder at the wonder boy, who seemed to find everything so easy? The real sickener for him must have been watching Piggott win the Derby at his third attempt. Gordon's first Derby triumph on Pinza the previous year – just after he received his knighthood – followed a string of twenty-seven failures in the event. And the other jockeys revered Richards – 'Gordon got away with murder; they would give him six lengths start out of the gate,' Lindley says. There was undoubtedly much ganging up against Lester on the old champion's behalf and at Royal Ascot it brought the lad a vicious blow that must have shaken even Gordon and his allies.

Piggott swallowed his medicine, as he would do so often in the future, with admirable dignity, even though the Ascot affair would rankle with him for years. He swapped a life of glamour for the role of a humble stable lad with the veteran trainer, Jack Jarvis, in Newmarket and was not even allowed to go racing as a spectator. Furthermore, from raking in the sort of money a city whiz-kid might expect, he was reduced to what he described as 'six months bloody hard labour and less than a fiver a week while serving it'.

Keith Piggott was quoted as saying: 'Lester is heart-broken. His whole life is racing. But I keep telling him that six months will seem nothing when compared with his tremendous future in the game.' In fact, some who knew the Piggott set-up have suggested that getting away from his father for a while was no bad thing for Lester. It appears that Piggott senior was rather too unrelenting in honing his son's talent, treating him rather like one of those pre-pubescent tennis prodigies who spring up so regularly nowadays and are burnt out before you can say 'Advantage, McEnroe'.

Missing the winning ride on Never Say Die in the St Leger two months after Ascot was another bitter pill for Lester, but he cheerfully gave Smirke some advice on how best to ride the colt. In any event the wheel of fortune was beginning to swing back inexorably in Piggott's favour. At the end of September the Jockey Club curtailed Piggott's sentence and allowed him to re-apply for his licence. He had to sweat buckets to reduce his ballooning weight, but his first ride back – on Cardington King at Newmarket – was a winner and the public, who had sympathised deeply with him, welcomed him back like a conquering hero.

Sir Gordon and his mates had tried every trick in the book to blot out the brightest star in the firmament, but inevitably they had failed. Lester was back and shooting for the moon.

CHAPTER TWO
MURLESS, MARRIAGE
AND MACHINATIONS

Lester Piggott has never been backward at coming forward. Perhaps his most significant professional trait has been a readiness to go out and grab what he wants as though it were his divine right to do so. Even at eighteen, still smarting from the Jockey Club's slap-down, he had no hesitation in picking up the phone to pop the most audacious question of his young life.

Shortly after Piggott had been sent packing by racing's ruling body, Gordon Richards was making his own exit from the riding scene, although in his case the departure was permanent. Sir Gordon, then aged fifty, had a heavy fall at Sandown and decided to retire, leaving a mouth-watering vacancy with Noel Murless at the magnificent Warren Place training establishment in Newmarket. (Richards, incidentally, asked Piggott to be his stable jockey when he set up as a trainer. Piggott turned the offer down, but remarked that the offer killed for ever the suggestion of any genuine feud between the two.) Incredibly, Murless received a cool 'Thanks, but no thanks' from several talented riders, among them the Australian, Scobie Breasley, who was to become one of Piggott's fiercest rivals during the next couple of decades. When Murless picked up the phone and heard Lester's nasal monotone on the other end asking him for the job, he was faced with what should have been a complex and heart-searching decision. It took him about thirty seconds to make up his mind.

The contrast between the two men could hardly have been greater. Murless, tall and supremely elegant in immaculate double-breasted suits, knife-edged trilby and highly polished brogues, was the imperious grand master of the training scene. With his military ways and strict adherence to old-fashioned discipline and values, he could be something of a martinet. Yet his bluff exterior concealed a soft centre. He would turn on an incompetent stable lad with terrible ferocity, but after threatening to sack him on the spot he might just as easily relent and then lend him a few pounds to help him out of a tight spot.

Murless's compassionate nature also revealed itself in the refreshingly enlightened approach he brought to his profession. When he took over the famous Beckhampton Stables from Fred Darling in 1947 before his move to Newmarket five years later, the business of training racehorses was still sullied by a high

Sir Noel Murless surveys his team of horses at exercise on the Heath. His prolific partnership with Piggott was to end in bitterness

degree of cruelty. Clive Brittain, currently one of England's leading trainers, worked for Murless for twenty-three years before setting up on his own no more than a short canter away, and he explains how Murless changed things dramatically for the better.

'Sir Noel was a breath of fresh air in the training ranks. In the old days horses could really get a thrashing. They used to employ "twisting up" jockeys, who were experts at laying into a horse with a whip. The horses would be down on their knees on the gallops trying to throw them off.

'In the days of Fred Darling, high-spirited horses would be secured by three rack chains to keep them from moving around their boxes. Sir Noel would allow only one chain. He also cut down on the ritualistic scrubbing and polishing of horses that so often resulted in sore skin. In effect he changed the whole system to make things easier for the staff and the horses.'

On the face of it, therefore, it might have seemed that a wild, whip-happy young rider like Piggott would be the last man Murless would consider. Bearing in mind that it was his responsibility to come up with a suitable successor to the seemingly irreplaceable Richards, one whom he could recommend to his august patrons, including the Queen, Sir Victor Sassoon and Prince Aly Khan, Murless's decision to employ Piggott was as brave as it was inspired. But Murless was as good a judge of men as he was of horses and he sensed the spark of true genius that fate had blown in his direction. When Noel signed up Lester he realised that all it needed was a little careful honing and channelling in the right direction to take the rough edges off the golden boy's whirlwind talent and convert it to greatness.

'When he first came to Warren Place, Lester was a wild kid doing everything wrong,' Brittain recalls. 'Sir Noel took him in hand and calmed him down. He told him that he didn't need to use his whip as if every post was a winning one. Noel adopted a fatherly approach to Lester and they helped one another. I cannot remember Lester ever saying one word against Noel – not that Lester would ever say anything bad about anyone – even after the partnership broke up.'

But Lester would not be Lester if he did not allow himself at least an irreverent thought or two, and it is worth recalling his well-chronicled first impression of Murless in working garb supervising his string on the Heath. 'His hat was one of the oldest I had seen. And as he led his string out to exercise I noticed his enormous feet and felt happy that I would never have to ride against him. For I thought that what looked like size 27s would only have to be turned outwards in the stirrups to make it impossible for anyone to pass him.'

Piggott was far too astute to put *his* big feet in it and spoil such a God-given opportunity. The relationship between the two complementary but entirely different types of genius flourished through mutual respect. In the eleven years they were in harness together, Murless consolidated his pre-eminence, adding four trainers' championships to his first in 1948 (he would win nine altogether).

And Piggott relentlessly asserted his superiority over the established names, although it was not until 1960 that he won the first of his eleven jockeys' titles.

Lift-off was certainly not instantaneous for the glittering new Murless–Piggott partnership, at least in terms of monopolising the major races. Nevertheless, during 1955, their first year together, Piggott finished third behind Doug Smith and Scobie Breasley in the jockeys' championship, having booted home 103 winners and, perhaps, more important, having managed to avoid even the smallest brush with the hawks of the Jockey Club. But the real significance of 1955 almost certainly escaped Lester as he saw out the old year vowing to leave Smith and Breasley trailing in his wake. Among the intake of yearlings at Warren Place that autumn was a spindly-legged chestnut colt owned by Sir Victor Sassoon. The colt, named Crepello, was an equine pearl, albeit a flawed one, and he was destined to overcome the impediments of nature and carry Piggott several giant strides further along his remarkable Epsom odyssey.

The flowering of Crepello, brief though it was, illustrated perfectly the unmatchable professional skills of both Murless and Piggott. Perhaps Murless's greatest quality as a trainer was his patience and understanding, although he set great store by getting horses as fit as possible at home. Brittain recalls him watching another trainer's string out at exercise on the Heath and commenting: 'Look at them. They look like a lot of fat old soldiers. You've got to be hard on horses.'

Murless's idea of being hard had nothing to do with severity, everything to do with a sensitively judged measure of physical exertion. There was never any question of forcing the horses to racing fitness unnaturally. Like the myriad of magnificent rose bushes that adorned the grounds of Warren Place, horses were nurtured with unstinting dedication and allowed to blossom in their own time. Only the greenest of fingers could have saved the unsound Crepello from ending up as a useless cripple.

For Piggott's part, it was his ability to cajole the absolute maximum out of a horse while inflicting the least damage that helped fashion Crepello into a dual Classic winner. Lester's kid-glove technique has always been unfairly over-shadowed by a preoccupation with his iron fist, but it is worth taking a brief look at the reality behind the distorted picture.

There can be no denying that Piggott could be extremely hard on a horse when the need arose and under the current guidelines on the use of the whip he would not have got away with some of the multi-stroke finishes he rode in his heyday. Although Murless insisted that Lester spare the rod, there was considerable outcry over the way he laid into certain horses during his period at Warren Place and on one occasion the RSPCA saw fit to complain over his riding of Casabianca at Newbury. The problem was one of appearances. When Piggott got to work with his whip a horse certainly knew it had been hit, but the punishment was not half as bad as it looked. Like it or not, a whip has always been an accepted part of a jockey's equipment – even the RSPCA condones its use in certain circumstances – and Lester knew how to use it to maximum effect but with minimum residual damage.

Newmarket trainer Robert Armstrong, who is the brother of Piggott's wife, Susan, is quick to ridicule the suggestion that his brother-in-law is in any way brutal, citing the example of a race at Doncaster when Piggott worked a near miracle on a rather reluctant filly that had driven the trainer to despair. 'I told Lester we desperately wanted her to win, it was her last chance,' Armstrong explains. 'He threw in everything and seemed to be hitting her non-stop throughout the last three furlongs. No one else could have won on her.

'The amazing thing was that the vet examined the filly afterwards and there wasn't a mark on her. That was one of Lester's many priceless assets. He could be hard, but he had the ability to wave his wand without being cruel.'

Fulke Johnson Houghton, the Blewbury trainer for whom Piggott rode so many outstanding horses, echoes a common feeling that because Lester knew exactly how and where to hit a horse he subjected them to far less abuse than many other jockeys who were less obvious with their punishment. 'Lester hit horses in the right place and they always retained their form after he gave them what appeared to be a hard race,' Johnson Houghton says. 'His stick would curl neatly under their tail and not hurt them excessively. Other jockeys, for example Scobie Breasley, could be far harder on them. Scobie would squeeze them and squeeze them and they wouldn't eat up afterwards.'

There were many occasions when Lester would eschew force altogether and bring the subtle touch of a concert violinist to his riding. That was how it was with Crepello.

Murless had forty colts in his yard in 1956, all big, strong individuals the way he liked them, and the powerful chestnut Crepello stood head and shoulders above them all in every way. 'When I first sat on him at home I knew at once he was special, a real powerhouse,' Clive Brittain recalls. 'He had a strong character, too, but the real problem was that he had so much power coming from behind that the phenomenal speed he generated put too much pressure on his front legs.

'He was a real man's ride. Jack Upton used to ride him in most of his work and I can still see him now exploding up the gallops with Jack on his back with his legs hanging right down like a policeman.'

When Lester took over for the serious business of the track he handled Crepello like a Ming vase, ensuring that those fragile forelegs would be subjected to minimum pressure. 'Lester is such a natural rider that he could balance his weight so a horse didn't even know he was on his back until he had to pressurise him,' Brittain says. 'Lester took the weight off Crepello's brittle forelegs and only allowed him to do just sufficient to win. Another jockey could well have broken Crepello down before or during the Derby.'

The road to Epsom was taken one tiptoeing step at a time. Crepello did not really show the spark of a champion as a juvenile, even though he fought his way to victory in one of the most important events in the calendar, the Dewhurst Stakes, on his third and final outing that season. Nevertheless, as the 1957 campaign approached, there was a new spring in Murless's step as he carried out his daily tours of inspection with a special eye on the handsome chestnut who he felt certain had the Classic prizes at his hooves. Those suspect front legs were always uppermost in Murless's mind, which meant Crepello's campaign would have to be orchestrated with extreme sensitivity, but there could not have been a better man to do the job.

Murless was the supreme artist when it came to getting a contender fit for a championship event without a preliminary bout. So when Lester whisked Crepello to post for what was then the first of the season's five Classics, the 2,000 Guineas at Newmarket (the 1,000 Guineas for fillies only is now run two days earlier) the colt was a heavily backed 7–2 chance. 'The lads couldn't get enough money on him for the 2,000 Guineas in the spring. They knew he was a dynamo,' Brittain says. Those who put their hard-earned cash down had little cause to reach for the brandy bottle until near the finish when Crepello, having cruised through from the rear into a decisive lead, decided he had done enough to justify his feed that night and eased off the throttle. He hung on, but Quorum and Pipe of Peace were lungeing menacingly at his flanks as they flashed past the post.

Not the performance of a great horse, but one that still had 'Derby' engraved on it in letters of gold, especially as Crepello was bred for distances well in excess of the Guineas mile. And to underline the feeling that Piggott only had to point Crepello in the right direction at Epsom to win, the colt suddenly began to produce searing form on the gallops. Confidence overflowed as Crepello became a red-hot 6–4 chance for Epsom. There had been a shadow hanging over the colt after a threat to dope him was received and security was drastically tightened. Jack Upton and Jim 'The Gunner', the lad who looked after Crepello, sat up all night with him before the race. Lester was so certain he would win, however, that he remarked: 'I don't know what the old man's worried about – he'll win anyway.' Crepello did not leave Warren Place for Epsom until the morning of the race. Many trainers like their horses to stay overnight so they can gallop on the course in the morning, but Murless had a theory that some horses will act round the bizarre circuit once, but not a second time, and therefore never exercised them on the track.

Crepello's Epsom performance was as smooth as it had been on the rolling green of Newmarket Heath. The horse proved conclusively that he was the champion Murless had always believed him to be, but the immaculate execution of the victory owed much to Piggott. With its endless succession of turns, gradients and cambers, Epsom is arguably the hardest course in the world to master. From first acquaintance Piggott rode it as if he were strolling round his own back yard. Ray Cochrane consulted Piggott on how best to tackle the track

Sir Victor Sassoon leads Crepello into the famous Epsom winner's circle after the colt had carried Piggott to his second Derby success in 1957. Crepello never ran again after the Derby as his suspect legs finally gave out

when he won his first Derby on Kahyasi in 1988. 'Epsom is a real bitch of a course, but Lester rides it brilliantly. He is unquestionably the king round there,' Cochrane says. 'With all the twists and gradients you have to be alive to problems every second. But Lester never makes mistakes because basically he is always in the right place at the right time.' So it was with Crepello. The positioning, the timing of the winning run, the economy of effort – Lester carried the whole thing off with an awe-inspiring fluidity. What is more, he subjected Crepello to the easiest race he could possibly have had, using negligible power to ease him home comfortably ahead of the Irish-trained colt Ballymoss, whose subsequent victories included the Irish Derby, St Leger, King George VI and Queen Elizabeth Stakes and Prix de l'Arc de Triomphe.

For Crepello the future ended then and there. He was due to run in the King George and Queen Elizabeth Stakes at Ascot, but when the ground turned into a bog Murless pulled him out, fearing the mud might put too much strain on Crepello's tendons. Shortly afterwards, the Derby hero pulled up lame at exercise and was retired. The public saw his flickering flame only five times, but Lester has never forgotten the raging fire inside. Crepello will always have a special place in the galaxy of great horses he rode.

There was an amusing postscript to Crepello's victory. It is a story that circulates from time to time in racing circles to perpetuate one of the Piggott myths – that of his alleged short arms and long pockets. As we shall see later, there is a wide divergence between myth and fact.

Sir Victor Sassoon, the owner of Crepello, was something of a rum character himself. Having inherited £15 million, he built on his fortune through astute international business dealing. He owned a bloodstock dynasty and yet while enjoying a sybaritic lifestyle appropriate to his title and position, when he stayed at the Ritz Hotel he insisted on laundering his own underwear.

Sir Victor had won the Derby with Pinza, but Crepello's victory gave him a special pleasure because he had bred the colt. He expressed his delight by giving Piggott a magnificently ostentatious Lincoln Continental. Soon after taking delivery, Lester invited Fulke Johnson Houghton's mother, Helen, who was like a second mother to him, for a spin in the splendid new vehicle. On the way Lester stopped at a garage for petrol, then informed the unsuspecting lady that he had left his wallet at home and tapped her for a loan!

Four days after Crepello's cruise, the young king of Epsom rode a race fit for a queen when he inched home in the royal colours to take the Oaks on Carrozza. Some say it was the finest race he has ever ridden. It certainly illustrated to the full Murless's most succinct tribute to Piggott's genius – that no one knew better exactly where the winning post was. Such an attribute might seem a prerequisite for any top jockey, but what Murless meant was that whether Piggott was riding a waiting race or outfoxing his rivals from the front, he knew precisely when to play his hand. The real trick of race riding is knowing how much a horse has left and

Command performance: The Queen greets her filly, Carrozza, after Piggott had produced a typically inspired finish to get her up in the final strides of the 1957 Oaks

deciding when to make the move that will win the race. Get there too soon and his energy may be prematurely dissipated, arrive too late and the consequence is obvious. Such errors simply did not figure in the Piggott manual of jockeyship.

When Piggott launched Carrozza into the lead early in the straight, the Oaks seemed over bar a fevered shouting that would have registered high on the Richter scale. Queen Elizabeth, who leased Carrozza from the National Stud, was about to land her first Classic winner and toppers were already in hand ready to be hurled into the air.

The hats were suddenly put on hold as the Irish-trained filly Silken Glider, galvanised by Jimmy Eddery (father of the current champion, Pat, and his successful brother, Paul) hunted Carrozza down. Eddery seemed certain to be guilty of *lèse-majesté* as he urged Silken Glider's head ever closer to the struggling

Carrozza's. Piggott moved into the drive position, his whip beating out a familiar tattoo. Still it seemed the Irish filly must go past. She did, but not until a couple of strides past the post. Lester seemed almost to stretch his mount's body as he somehow kept her ahead by the width of a flaring nostril.

The Queen *was* amused. She simply beamed with delight, waving her hands excitedly as Piggott lifted Carrozza over the line. Lester had made the ultimate friend in high places, but sadly she would never be able to bestow on him the supreme reward of a knighthood. A devoted fan of Piggott throughout the rest of his career, the Queen would dearly have loved to say 'Arise, Sir Lester,' but she was to be deprived of the pleasure by Piggott's financial folly and her servants in the Inland Revenue and Customs and Excise departments.

Two years later Lester was associated with another young queen, the magnificent Murless filly Petite Etoile, whose towering talent provided the perfect showcase for the full range of Lester's artistry. Ironically, Piggott's usually immaculate judgement cost him the first major prize of Petite Etoile's career, in the 1,000 Guineas. He rejected her in favour of another Murless filly, Collyria, owned by Sir Victor Sassoon – one of the few major errors of his career – and watched miserably from the rear as Doug Smith, wearing Prince Aly Khan's green and brown hooped silks, urged Petite Etoile home in front of the cream of the year's fillies.

Given the same choice for the Oaks the following month, Lester did not hesitate. Nudging Petite Etoile past the post three lengths ahead of Cantelo (winner of the St Leger later in the season), he marked the beginning of one of racing's most memorable partnerships. Their subsequent triumphs included the Sussex Stakes, Yorkshire Oaks, Champion Stakes and two Coronation Cups (Aly Khan was killed in a car crash shortly after the first in 1960). It was the impudent manner of those victories that captured the imagination of the racing public and made Lester and the grey *femme fatale* of the track as much of a drawing card, even for non-racing folk, as Desert Orchid has been in recent years.

'Lester rode Petite Etoile with such confidence. He made her 7lb better than any other jockey could have done,' Brittain says. 'She didn't really stay a mile and a half even though she won the Oaks, but Lester conserved her finishing speed so well. It was marvellous to see him cruising in behind the others and then cutting them down at the death.'

Piggott's extraordinary *sang-froid* sometimes caused connections and backers of Petite Etoile to reach for the valium. In the Champion Stakes, Lester appeared to get himself snookered even though he had only two rivals, the French-trained colt Javelot and the Irish challenger Barclay, whose rider headed Piggott off when Piggott initially went to challenge between the other two. But such minor irritations do not worry Lester. Even though the post was looming rapidly, he merely sat back and waited for a second go. While the other two doubtless expected him to pull round the outside, Piggott calmly popped Petite Etoile up

Prince Aly Khan leads Petite Etoile back after her victory in the Oaks of 1959. Piggott and the brilliant grey filly made a spectacular partnership, but Lester's last-minute challenges did not always meet with the owner's approval

through the middle near the line and stole the prize by half a length. Aly Khan, watching from his box, looked about as happy as a chicken with an invitation to a Colonel Sanders barbecue and duly informed Murless of his displeasure. But Murless had such confidence in Piggott that he simply shrugged his shoulders and said: 'That's Lester. He wasn't beaten.'

The following summer, even Murless could not calm the storm that followed Petite Etoile's narrow defeat by Aggressor in Ascot's King George VI and Queen Elizabeth Stakes. As usual, Lester asked Petite Etoile to come from a long way off the pace. This time she didn't quite make it and was half a length behind Jimmy Lindley's mount, Aggressor, at the line.

The criticism levelled at Piggott was undoubtedly unfair. Brittain says that

Lester could have done no more: Aggressor was a relentless galloper and ran the finish out of the filly – and Scobie Breasley later admitted to making things difficult for Lester in revenge for another incident. But it is Geoff Lewis, the former hotel pageboy who rode over 2,300 winners worldwide and was nicknamed 'Flip' by the other jockeys because of his habit of saying 'Flipping this' and 'Flipping that', who steps in with the most solid defence of his old weighing-room buddy, providing conclusive proof that Piggott had a raw deal. 'I was riding Kythnos for Paddy Prendergast in the King George and wanted to finish as close as I could even if I couldn't win. In the straight I felt I would run into a place [he finished third] and when Lester wanted me to let him out I wouldn't. When he finally got through it was too late.

'The incredible thing was that Lester didn't say an angry word to me afterwards. If he'd done that to me I'd have wanted to hit him. The reason he gave for Petite Etoile's defeat was that the grass was too long. However, he did get his own back when he "levelled" me at Kempton three weeks later. I was riding an old horse called Red Letter and Lester knocked into me so hard I ended up facing the wrong way and almost went over the rail.'

While Piggott's riding of Petite Etoile thrilled millions, it also irritated some, and there were doubtless many harsh words from angry punters after the filly's King George defeat. Piggott's nonchalant style, particularly when he left it so late, made him an obvious target for the cynics, who saw a darker side to his genius, as Brittain explains. 'Lester made horses look better than they were. He was such a poker player. Nobody knew what he was up to. He would leave the others open-mouthed when he suddenly quickened up or made an unexpected move. But because of his style and the fact that sometimes he would suddenly ease off the throttle, he got accused of deliberately stopping so many horses. Those stories were all rubbish, he was saving the horses.'

The Jockey Club, who had eased up on Lester for a few years, clearly thought there was more to his riding of Ione at Lincoln in May 1962 than mere consideration for a beaten horse. Ione was trained in Staffordshire by Bob Ward, who was generally regarded as something of a sharp merchant, and when Lester came home second on Ione, beaten by Ward's other runner, Polly Macaw, the stewards decided to pounce. Ward was banned for eight years; Piggott's licence was suspended for two months, ruling him out of the Derby and Royal Ascot. The sentence was another piece of rough justice from the men of the Jockey Club that burned in Lester's memory for years.

Lots more happened to Lester during the rest of his stint at Warren Place, not all of it bad by any means. He won another Derby on St Paddy in 1960 and lifted his second jockeys' championship in 1964, beginning a straight run of eight titles. Even by Piggott's standards that third Derby triumph was a breeze, but it also represented another little gem of empathy and persuasion by the young virtuoso of the saddle.

Piggott canters to his third Epsom triumph on St Paddy in 1960

St Paddy, owned like Crepello by Sir Victor Sassoon, was a devil of a horse with a supercharged engine and a mind of his own. Piggott and Brittain were the only two who could ride him at home. He tore off so fast that no one else was able to hold him. 'St Paddy was such a terrific puller that he'd leave bumps on your arms like walnuts,' Brittain says. 'Lester never fought him, that was the secret. Instead of trying to hold him up he got him to settle in front. St Paddy could be as sweet natured as anything, but if you upset him he could be a terror. After he won the Derby he was so wound up that we had to stop the horsebox on the way home and take him out for a while. Something bugged him and if we hadn't let him out he would have kicked the box to pieces.' Later that year St Paddy carried Piggott to the first of eight victories in the season's final Classic, the St Leger, which he also took the following year on another Murless horse, Aurelius.

Piggott will always believe that he would have won Derby number four on Pinturischio, another Sassoon horse, had this potentially brilliant colt not been doped twice in the weeks leading up to Epsom. It was an open secret that a firm of bookmakers had bribed one of the stable lads to nobble the colt, who carried a welter of ante-post cash. Piggott reacted by saying: 'People who dope horses should be shot. Travelling at speed on a doped horse is highly dangerous. If a jockey was killed the villains who nobbled the horse should be tried for manslaughter.'

Piggott might well have been fatally injured himself when he suffered a horrendous fall riding Persian Garden for Murless at Longchamp. The accident occurred in September 1964, when Lester was busy fighting off two dogged Australians, Ron Hutchinson and Scobie Breasley, who had won the championship the three previous years, on the way to his second title. Persian Garden, racing in the middle of the field, was squeezed out and fell; two horses behind came down on top of Lester, who was rushed unconscious to the Clinique Jouvenet at St Cloud. The toll of serious bruising and lacerations, plus a legacy of severe headaches, was a lot less than it might have been. He was expected to be out for the season, but knowing that a couple of hungry 'crocs' from down under were snapping ever closer at his heels, he exhibited typical stoicism to make it back to the saddle in three weeks.

Lester's long-standing friend Charles St George, for whom he rode many outstanding horses, visited Lester in hospital and remembered how his dry sense of humour showed through, even though he looked as if he had collided head-on with a juggernaut. 'Lester had been given a suppository for the pain and he made as if to pop it in his mouth. The nurse told him "Non, monsieur" and pointed to his bottom. Lester grinned and said "It's too late. I've swallowed two already."'

That sort of wry, off-beat humour, glimpsed all too rarely by outsiders, was one of the qualities that attracted Susan Armstrong to Lester and helped to forge a relationship that was sealed when they married on 22 February 1960, in front of a small gathering of friends and relatives in London. Lester, looking like a young matinee idol with his sleeked-back hair and lean good looks, was twenty-four. Susan, radiant in floral ensemble, was four years younger. It was a pairing that provided the ideal recipe for marital harmony – he wore the breeches and she wore the trousers. That might sound unduly harsh on Susan, but there is no doubt that while Lester was very much his own man, she did a fair bit of back-seat manoeuvring on major issues, such as his decision to give up riding and become a trainer.

As the daughter of a leading Newmarket trainer, Sam Armstrong, and an accomplished amateur rider, Susan's background was perfect for Lester. Later on in their marriage she developed her own highly successful bloodstock agency. She presented Lester with two daughters: Maureen, who is married to Newmarket

Lester and Susan at their wedding in London in 1960. They were both very private people not given to displays of emotion and one writer suggested that they communicated by tic-tac

trainer Willie Haggas, and Tracy, who is an up-and-coming television commentator.

Susan's culinary cleverness helped Lester cope with the vicious hunger pangs that still assailed him in the early part of his career. She also performed another important service for her megastar husband – helping to keep the world off his back. Ask any media man who has tried to arrange an interview with Lester. A few well-chosen words from the sharp-tongued Susan can send even the most hard-bitten of journalists scurrying away like a frightened rabbit.

Susan shared many personality traits and attitudes with Lester. For example, among the things she said during an interview with Angela Levin in the *Mail on Sunday* recently were the following: 'On the whole I think horses are much nicer than people. Unless they are given cause to be bad-tempered or spiteful, they won't be . . . I don't like talking about feelings . . . Neither of us is extroverted . . . I was always a bit of a loner. I don't remember having a normal social life as a child . . . I can't stand waste of any sort. That was instilled into me by my father.' That could easily have been Lester talking.

One of Susan's main grouses was the persistence of the myths that clung to Lester, particular those alleging meanness and a miserable nature. 'Why on earth do people have the idea that Lester is an untalkative misery?' she once said. 'He can be very funny and often has us all creased up with his dry wit. It is also ridiculous to suggest he is some sort of mean old Scrooge-like character. He is perfectly free with money and behaves the way any loving husband and father would, particularly when it comes to handing out presents.' Susan also told Angela Levin of her fears about Lester being injured. 'Lester has had many fairly horrific accidents. I've never got used to them, but they've enabled me to build up a mechanism to shield me from reality. It's a terrible shock each time he's had an accident and actually a lot worse than what has happened to him recently [referring to Lester's imprisonment].'

The late Jean Rook, columnist on the *Daily Express*, once said of Susan: 'She is reputed to be as taciturn as Lester and some people say they communicate by tic-tac.' They certainly had their problems, limping through several bad patches, but then what couple hasn't? Their relationship has stood the test of time, which was more than could be said for Piggott's partnership with Noel Murless. That began to creak ominously towards the mid-sixties when Lester's wandering eyes sought out new conquests.

As Piggott grew ever more successful and dominant at the highest level, his hunger for winners became an insatiable lust. More and more winners were coming from outside Warren Place through Piggott's ever-increasing circle of contacts and his encyclopaedic knowledge of the horses, their capabilities and their potential availability. That famous picture of the young, chubby-cheeked Lester avidly reading the racing weekly, *The Winner*, provided a far more accurate clue to Lester's preoccupation than his much-talked-about daily perusal of the *Financial Times* and his alleged obsession with finance and investment. Piggott's knowledge of the form book and his judgement of which horse to ride in a particular race was uncanny, and that included horses trained abroad: Lester would constantly amaze his colleagues on journeys overseas by apprising them of the precise details of the latest foreign form.

Mark Beecroft, who rode with a fair degree of success in the north before becoming senior race-riding instructor at the British School of Racing, recalls a typical example of the way Piggott homed in on even the humblest of winners with radar-like precision. 'When I was a young apprentice claiming a 7lb

A winner on form: Piggott's encyclopaedic knowledge of racing was one of his greatest assets. Here the young Lester gets down to some serious study

allowance I was due to ride a horse for the northern trainer, Bob Harmon, at Newcastle one Bank Holiday,' Beecroft explains. 'Lester rang Bob up out of the blue and said: "I'd like to ride that horse of yours. He'll win." Bob told Lester that he would prefer to keep me on board because my allowance would knock 7lb off the weight the horse was set to carry.

'Lester came up to me before the race and said: "You'll win this, son." The horse won all right and Lester finished fourth. He came up to me again in the weighing room afterwards and said "I told you he'd win." When you think that it was just about the weakest selling race in the calendar, it shows you how incredible his knowledge and judgement was.'

Equally impressive was Lester's inside information on what went on behind the closed stable doors and proliferation of hedgerows and walls in training centres that are built to keep horses in and prying eyes out. His intelligence network made MI5 look like a bunch of schoolboy snoopers. He appeared to know exactly who was riding what in the early-morning sorties on the gallops, which ones were worth pursuing as possible mounts, and probably what their lads had eaten for breakfast as well.

Bruce Raymond, the veteran jockey currently enjoying a marvellous resurgence in his career, explains: 'Lester would be walking round the weighing room, then he'd suddenly plonk himself down next to you and say something like: "Here, you know that two-year-old you rode this morning."

'You'd reply: "What two-year-old?" and Lester would say: "You know, that colt by The Minstrel with the white blaze."

'You'll think to yourself, "How the bloody hell did he know about that?" and then he'll ask: "How did he go?"

'You end up telling him and the next thing you know you're off the horse and he's on it!'

Raymond, who has a massive portrait of Lester taking pride of place in the living room of his Newmarket home, adds: 'All the jockeys have a sort of love-hate relationship with Lester. They know exactly what he gets up to, but they regard him as a sort of God. Everyone tells him everything he wants to know just because he's Lester.'

Piggott was like a kid in a sweet shop trying to grab every giant bar of chocolate and stuff them all into his satchel before anyone else could get at them. And quantity alone was not enough. He especially wanted to get on the cream of the world's Thoroughbred population in the prestige events. That often spelled frustration, however, because he was committed to Murless, whose genius did not extend to sending out the winner of every big race that was run.

Julie Cecil, Sir Noel's daughter and now training successfully herself, recalls how Lester would always give his feelings away when he came into the house at Warren Place with a lot more than idle chit-chat on his mind. 'When Lester came in he would spend most of his time nicking the chocolates. Sometimes he would

On the phone or in a plane, Piggott's quest
for winners all over the world was relentless

just sit in the sitting room and say nothing and we knew something was wrong, like he'd been suspended. At other times he would sit on the window seat in the sitting room and kick his legs, which meant he wanted to be let off riding one of father's horses.'

The result of Lester's ceaseless manoeuvring and machinations was an increasing tension in his relationship with Murless, for whom absolute loyalty was a prerequisite. During 1966 the writing was on the stable wall when Piggott chose to dispense with his retainer from Murless, but carried on riding for him. The crunch came in the Oaks of that year when Lester opted to ride Valoris for the Irish trainer, Vincent O'Brien, in preference to Varinia from the Murless yard. Valoris skated home with Varinia in third place. The Murless–Piggott partnership limped on for a while, but Murless had been cut to the quick by Lester's action and after further slights from the champion jockey, he announced that enough was enough. Lester could go take a hike.

'We have been together for many years and had many notable successes, but I had to take this stand,' Murless said. 'Lester was simply not going to play ducks and drakes with me. I have no regrets at my decision.'

Piggott's shenanigans outraged many racing folk, among them the leading Irish trainer, Paddy Prendergast, for whom Piggott had been riding top-class horses for some two years. 'I would never engage Piggott again under any circumstances. Not for the crown jewels of England,' Prendergast said.

Lester shrugged off these stinging rebuffs and looked with confidence to the future. During 1966 some 80 per cent of his winners had come from outside Warren Place. What need did he have of a retainer when he could pick and choose from many of the best stables in Europe? Riding freelance was almost unprecedented for a top jockey, but with the sort of ammunition he could call on, Piggott regarded the move more as a blue-chip investment than as a gamble.

So, in 1967, the dawn of a new era arrived. Lester was out on his own in every sense. In the beginning, however, he found life as the lone ranger anything but an easy ride.

CHAPTER THREE
THE WHISPERING DOCTOR AND THE ROAR OF THE CROWD

Few men have been as handsomely placed to make a quick killing as Mick Hinchliffe. As chauffeur to Lester Piggott for eleven years during the sixties and seventies, Hinchliffe could virtually have named his price to reveal the intimate secrets about the eleven times champion jockey that he came to share during that time. Yet Hinchliffe, who now runs a successful horse transport business in Berkshire, has declined a string of lucrative offers from newspapers and publishers. Cash has not corrupted his innate sense of loyalty and fair play and he has steadfastly refused to divulge anything but the merest sliver of his reminiscences until now.

In talking to me about the hundreds of hours spent on the road with Lester, Hinchliffe was still very guarded. Nevertheless, he did provide a few intriguing little vignettes that offer further insight into Piggott's character.

'I was already chauffeuring several jockeys including Greville Starkey, Frank Durr and Bill Rickaby on a freelance basis and I turned down Lester's offer of a retainer when he first approached me in 1966,' Hinchliffe recalls. 'Eventually I decided to accept a retainer from him in February 1967, when he was just starting out as a freelance. At that time Lester had a big old Austin Westminster before he changed to a Mercedes.

'I suppose if you add up all the hours we spent travelling together, I was with him more than his wife. And in those eleven years we only ever had two rows, one of which was my fault. I remember he would always take an old blue mac with a toasted sandwich in it. That was his meal twenty minutes before racing. Despite what people said, he did eat and on the way home he was always getting me to stop so he could buy chocolates and ice cream. And of course he was always puffing away at those big cigars.

'People always go on about Lester's meanness, but that is unfair. It is true that he disliked spending money and had something of an obsession about it. He trusted no one where money was concerned. That was the thing I found most strange about him. But he always paid me on time and I found him a generous man to work for. I remember once taking him to Heathrow when he was riding in France. He told me to wait for him and pick him up in the evening and he gave

Although he loved fast cars, limousines were not always part of Lester's life. Here he and Susan set off in their ageing Austin Westminster

me £15, which was a lot in those days, to get a meal for myself and my wife and kids. He said go and have a drive round Windsor and enjoy yourself.

'In all the years I drove him he never showed any emotion before or after a race, whether he was riding in a Classic or a little seller. It was just a job to him, a job that he found so easy. He did have a particular affection for Sir Ivor [of whom more later in this chapter]. I'm sure he was Lester's favourite horse of all time.

'You could not help but admire him, he was so totally dedicated. When he retired I told everybody "I can't see the point of this. He can't do anything other than ride." He should never have stopped.'

Hinchliffe says that Lester had only two topics of conversation when they were whizzing to and from meetings – horse racing and cars, which Lester liked driven as fast as possible. 'We had to go everywhere like stink. We once did Newmarket to Heathrow in an hour and three minutes on a Sunday.' When Piggott got behind the wheel himself, he was a demon driver. Friends will tell you that he puts his foot down and keeps it down, frequently ignores traffic lights, one-way signs and anything else that gets in his way and has only one aim – to get from A to B in the shortest possible time. Frightening though this was to the uninitiated, Piggott was an exceptionally skilled driver. Robert Armstrong, Piggott's brother-in-law, who is a motor-racing enthusiast, says: 'Lester was one of the most impressive drivers of a car I've ever seen. If he'd gone into motor racing he would definitely have made it to the top. He had the most wonderful reactions.'

It was not so much Piggott's reactions as those of his white-knuckled passengers that figure in two lovely little stories from Hinchliffe. The first concerns an occasion when he was riding in the first race at Newbury and asked Hinchliffe to go on ahead from Newmarket and meet him at Baldock. Lester had business to discuss with his old friend, the wealthy racehorse owner Charles St George, and said he would follow behind in St George's car. St George was on his way to London, and the idea was that he would drop Lester off in Baldock, where Hinchliffe would pick him up and drive him to Newbury.

It all went wrong when two other jockeys hitched a ride to Newbury with Hinchliffe, who assured them that Piggott would not mind. Because of this unscheduled stop Hinchliffe got some way behind St George's car, was unable to spot him en route and failed to make contact at the appointed meeting place. Because one of the other jockeys, Frank Durr, was also riding in the first race, Hinchliffe decided to go straight to the course. Meanwhile, St George had taken Piggott on to London where he arranged for a taxi to take him to Newbury.

'Lester decided that the taxi driver wasn't going fast enough, so he took over,' Hinchliffe explains. 'The taxi driver was so scared by Lester's driving that he ended up on the floor, unable to look. In the meantime we had arrived at Newbury and Frank Durr took Lester's mac with the toasted sandwich in it to the weighing room.

'I waited at the Members' entrance for Lester as usual. When he came out after racing he slung his bag in the boot and said "You're a bugger, aren't you. You went past us at a hundred miles an hour." After that the whole thing was forgotten. He never said another word about it.'

The other tale concerns the wealthy Armenian owner, Souren Vanian, who owned a stud in Newmarket and for whom Piggott rode regularly in France. After racing at Newmarket one Saturday, on the eve of the Prix de l'Arc de Triomphe, Vanian accepted a lift from Lester to Stansted airport. 'Vanian was in the front and Lester said to me "Kick on,"' Hinchliffe recounts. 'He was an enormous man and when we picked up speed he started to sweat and held on to the dashboard. We took a bend too fast and ended up on the grass verge. Vanian, whose face was white by this time, banged his hand on the dashboard and said "Better to arrive late than never to arrive at all."

'Several times after that Lester sent me to pick him up when he was coming over to England, but he would never ride with me again. In fact he ended up paying me not to drive him!'

During those eleven years, Hinchliffe saw Piggott's career carry him ever higher to a point where he became one of the most celebrated and wealthy sportsmen in the world. But there were also one or two spectacular lows, and

George Moore, seen here with his two sons, enjoyed a fantastic run of success when he took over from Piggott as stable jockey to Sir Noel Murless. Death threats forced the Australian rider to return home after only one season, however

none worse than those first few months of the 1967 season when Lester's decision to go freelance looked like the most injudicious move he had ever made.

It had all seemed so straightforward. Piggott had every right to assume that he would be inundated with requests from trainers and owners and be able to pick and choose the cream. That was the theory, but the winners simply would not come. At one point he was really being put through the wringer, enduring an unprecedented losing run of thirty-one and watching bookmakers double his odds for the championship. Many felt that the slump heralded the beginning of the end for Lester, at least at the very highest level, and that he would never be champion again.

What made the outlook far worse for Piggott was the fact that Murless began the season in the most sensational way. The trainer had brought over the Australian jockey, George Moore, to replace Piggott and the new partnership could do no wrong. They took the 2,000 and 1,000 Guineas with Royal Palace and

Fleet and then Moore pushed the knife in further when he drove home Royal Palace in the Derby with Piggott finishing second on Ribocco. Lester was really suffering, as Hinchliffe reveals.

'Loyalty was considered paramount in racing and because of the Murless affair people were shunning Lester. We were driving to meetings for just one ride a day. Nothing was going right and Lester was getting really depressed.

'I remember one day we went to Sandown for just one ride and afterwards Lester came out, slung his bag in the boot and said "Have you seen that George Moore ride? His arse keeps hitting the saddle. I think I'm going to have to try that."'

They say you cannot keep a good man down and by the same token it takes an act of God to shackle a great one. Slowly but inexorably Piggott hauled himself back from the depths and his resurgence was completed in the sweetest way when he taunted Moore with the most arrogant of victories in the Irish Derby at the Curragh. Moore was aboard the Murless runner, Sucaryl, and having swept into the lead some way from the finish the Australian must have felt he had another plum prize in his tucker bag. Had he looked behind him, however, he would have seen Piggott on Ribocco, bottom pointing skywards, poised to cut him down like a cheetah stalking a gazelle. There can have been few sweeter moments in Lester's career than the dozen or so flowing strides when Ribocco surged past Sucaryl. As Charles Engelhard's colt strode ahead Lester glanced across at Moore with a look that needed no words to embellish it.

The sheer ecstasy showed afterwards when Piggott, in a spontaneous gesture of emotion, embraced Ribocco and gave him a huge kiss. Robert Armstrong recalls Lester doing the same thing to the brilliant Moorestyle after the colt had won the final race of his prolific career in Paris. 'Lester jumped down from Moorestyle, gave him a kiss on the nose and whispered "Thanks for the memory". It was a magical moment,' Armstrong says. Another smack in the eye for anyone who believed that Piggott treated all horses as machines.

As for those who thought Piggott was a has-been before the Irish Derby, they were eating humble pie by the basinful before the season was out. Moore, aboard Murless's brilliant four-year-old, Busted, hammered Piggott and Ribocco to defeat in the King George VI and Queen Elizabeth Stakes; but the final thrust came from Lester when he produced Ribocco with an exquisite late flourish in the St Leger to deprive Moore on Hopeful Venture of a fourth English Classic. Piggott went on to retain his title, albeit with a greatly reduced total of 117. He was quoted as saying: 'Being champion again this year means so much to me in terms of satisfaction. The money is unimportant. Racing is such a fickle game and it is good to put those who wrote me off in their place.'

Piggott's successes on Ribocco were the start of a remarkable association with the American owner Charles Engelhard. A huge man who made his fortune in platinum dealing, Engelhard was an insomniac with a penchant for talking all night, drinking Coca Cola until it came out of his ears and shelling out big bucks for offspring of the unbeaten Italian champion, Ribot. The year after Ribocco's Classic successes, his full brother, Ribero, brought off the same Irish Derby–St Leger double. Piggott's tender persuasion on Ribero in the St Leger ranks as another contender for the best race he has ever ridden. Fulke Johnson Houghton, trainer of Ribocco and Ribero, still savours the memory.

'Ribero had an abscess in his mouth which burst the night before the Leger. It was touch and go whether he would run until the morning of the race,' Johnson Houghton explains. 'Lester was absolutely brilliant. Bill Williamson looked sure to go past him on Canterbury, but Lester never touched Ribero with the whip and just lifted him over the line. It was quite remarkable to watch. It was Lester at his very best – that and when the bugger beat me with The Minstrel in the Derby [Johnson Houghton trained the runner-up, Hot Grove].'

The Engelhard–Johnson Houghton–Piggott combination appeared to have another champion son of Ribot on their hands in Ribofilio, who looked a cut above the juvenile class of '68. Ribofilio started favourite for four Classics, but second place in the Irish Derby and St Leger was the nearest he came to upholding the family honour. Johnson Houghton is convinced the colt was doped before the 2,000 Guineas, in which he was pulled up after 100 yards.

Johnson Houghton also stresses that there was far more to Piggott's excellence than his riding. 'Apart from his brilliance in the saddle, Lester was right so often in his judgement of horses that it was bloody infuriating,' he says.

'He was a particularly good judge of a horse's best distance. For example, after he rode Double Form in the Greenham he told me the horse didn't stay and I didn't believe him. I ran him in the Guineas anyway and Lester was absolutely right. He turned out to be a champion sprinter. Lester also convinced me that Habitat was a miler, not a stayer, and sure enough he proved to be a champion at the shorter trip.

'The only time I remember him being wrong was when he turned down the winning ride on Ile de Bourbon in the King George. And the only bad race he ever rode for me was on Rose Bowl in the 1,000 Guineas. He made a balls of it and got shut in. After that she and Lester never really got on and Willie Carson took over.'

Piggott's off-the-cuff wit also endeared him to Johnson Houghton. 'I remember after he rode Ribocco in the Washington International at Laurel we were invited to a big reception at the French Embassy. It was an extremely pompous affair and Lester and I were lined up to come down the grand staircase to be introduced to some dignitaries. When it was our turn he whispered to me, "Shall we hold hands?" I nearly collapsed.'

Another of the trainer's memories was playing chauffeur. 'Lester had lost his licence and I would often drive him to meetings. It was in the days when they didn't have saunas at racecourses to help jockeys sweat off those last few pounds.

He would put on a rubber sweat suit, close the windows and turn the heater full on. I was nearly down to my underpants.'

So, after that faltering start, Piggott's freelance gamble was indeed proving the licence to print money that he had anticipated. The rich vein of Ribot gold petered out, but that did not bother him in the slightest. He already had an equine Fort Knox at his disposal in the shape of the fabled Ballydoyle stables in Co. Tipperary, masterminded by the extraordinary Dr Doolittle of the racing world, Vincent O'Brien, whose wide-ranging genius exceeded even that of Murless.

Piggott had no formal contract with O'Brien, but the two men had tied an unofficial knot when Piggott booted home O'Brien's good filly, Gladness, in the 1958 Ascot Gold Cup. That was how it stayed for the best part of twenty years until the arrival of the third man, Robert Sangster, on the scene (see Chapter Five). The Classic dominance achieved by the O'Brien–Piggott partnership in the late sixties and seventies was and still is unique in modern Flat racing.

O'Brien's story is the stuff of fiction. His father was a farmer who trained horses on the side and when he died Vincent rented the gallops from his half brother, who inherited everything. His upwardly mobile path was greatly assisted by a remarkable succession of gambling coups. He began with £4 from the sale of a greyhound bitch he bred, put it on a 10–1 winner and never looked back, hitting the bookmakers hard and often and totting up huge annual profits on a regular basis.

O'Brien's big-race haul since the war seems almost unreal. What puts him way above anyone else is the fact that his ascendancy was equally pronounced on the Flat and over jumps. No other trainer has remotely approached his achievements. His list of 'majors' includes three successive Grand Nationals, three successive Champion Hurdles, four Cheltenham Gold Cups, six Derbys, an overall total of sixteen English Classics and a hatful of other prestige events, including a phenomenal strike rate at Royal Ascot.

With his somewhat austere expression, priest-like bearing and natural reserve, he is a man who has always remained something of a closed book, and that in itself added to the aura of mystery that surrounded him. 'I'm afraid I'm very much an introvert,' he told Paul Haigh in the *Racing Post*. 'I'd love to be an extrovert, the sort of person who's the life and soul of the party. They have a much better time don't they?' That is very much a matter of opinion. The Whispering Doctor, as he is known (he received an Honorary LLD from the National University of Ireland in 1983), was born with the sort of gift that most mortals can only dream about. His rapport with animals of all kinds is uncanny. Dogs, cats, rabbits – almost any species will come to him when he calls them as if under some hypnotic spell. O'Brien's Australian wife, Jacqueline, once told me: 'Vincent has an amazing capacity for predicting animals' behaviour. When we used to go hunting he could always tell where the fox was going to make for.'

Vincent's perception and understanding of the Thoroughbred horse defied logical explanation. He would tell you that his ability unerringly to pick out the embryo champion from a gaggle of spindly-legged yearlings involved such things as conformation, good heart room, an intelligent head and a kind eye. But that scientific explanation does not tell even part of the story. O'Brien had an ability to look down into the very depths of a young horse's soul and sense where a spark of greatness lurked within a puny frame.

During O'Brien's rise to prominence there was much cynical talk about the methods he was using to achieve his unprecedented levels of success. Most of it was motivated by jealousy, as has been the case with the current National Hunt phenomenon, Martin Pipe. However, the doubters seemed to be supported by an incident involving one of O'Brien's horses, Chamour, who was found to have traces of an illegal drug in his system after winning a small race at the Curragh in April 1960. Chamour went on to win the Irish Derby, but Vincent was not around to enjoy it. He had been banned for eighteen months by the Irish Turf Club, who subsequently reduced the sentence to twelve months when they acknowledged publicly: 'The stewards did not find that Mr Vincent O'Brien had administered the drug or stimulant or knew of its administration.'

O'Brien's link-up with Piggott was like a great love affair. The two men were made for each other, in professional terms at any rate. They did not always see eye to eye, but they understood racehorses like no other men on earth. Watching these two racing superbrains huddled together in the paddock before a big race, plotting the execution of another great triumph, made you feel privileged to be a part of their era.

Vincent gave me the following evaluation of Lester: 'Down through the years racing enthusiasts have argued which was the greatest jockey, Lester or Fred Archer. Not having seen Archer riding I could not answer this, but I have been fortunate not only to see Lester's brilliant riding throughout his career but to have had his invaluable assistance riding for me over the years.

'As a jockey he is completely dedicated to his profession. He is ice cool under pressure, has a great empathy with his horses, he goes to all possible lengths to assess the ability of the opponents and thinks long and hard how he will beat them. He is a strategist – an analyst before and after the race as well as during it.'

In Raymond Smith's biography of the trainer, Piggott says of O'Brien: 'He was totally dedicated. For every minute of the day, he put his mind into the responsibilities of training . . . Perhaps the greatest tribute I can pay him is this: if the horses that he put through his hands were good, he got the very best out of them. If certain horses were no good, you might never even see them on a racecourse. It wasn't Vincent's way to waste time trying to unearth ability where he knew there was none, having given them every chance.'

The victory of Valoris in the 1966 Oaks, which brought about the final split in Piggott's relationship with Noel Murless, was the first Classic strike for the O'Brien–Piggott partnership: two years later came the first of a series of superhorses that lifted the combination on to another plane. The colt in question was named Sir Ivor and his spectacular exploits around the racetracks of the world, illuminated by the extraordinary artistry of Piggott, were so captivating that they were made into a prize-winning film, *The Year of Sir Ivor*.

In the last couple of decades there has been a change in the career patterns of Classic horses. Nowadays there is a growing belief that a strenuous juvenile career may prejudice the transition to full-blown three-year-old star. Thus we frequently see horses unheard of as youngsters graduating with honours in the Classic class of the following year. Michael Stoute, the three-times champion trainer, puts it this way. 'I am not against two-year-old racing for its own sake. It doesn't necessarily prejudice a horse's three-year-old career, but the policy has changed. We live in an age of specialisation. People are realising that horses bred to go middle distances do not always benefit from being highly tried as two-year-olds.' If you had tried telling that to O'Brien in his heyday he would have replied, in the most gentlemanly way, of course, that you were speaking a load of claptrap. O'Brien's great horses, like Sir Ivor, Nijinsky and The Minstrel, were all champion juveniles who translated the flashing brilliance of their first season into majestic supremacy the following year.

So it was with Sir Ivor, the American-bred colt who carved himself a unique place in Piggott's affections. Sir Ivor's brilliance shone out as a two-year-old and when he completed a hat-trick by pulverising the best of the French juveniles in the Grand Criterium at Longchamp in the autumn of 1967, even Lester was stirred beyond his normal monosyllabic reaction. 'His acceleration when I let him go in the straight was so fantastic that he almost shot out from underneath me. I knew straight away he was something special,' Piggott said.

Even knowing the sky-high opinion that both O'Brien and Piggott held of Sir Ivor there was much raising of eyebrows when Lester chose to ride Sir Ivor in the 2,000 Guineas the following spring in preference to the English-trained Petingo, who was considered one of the best horses to have winged across Newmarket Heath for many years. Piggott's decision was deemed even more controversial because Petingo was trained by his brother-in-law, Robert Armstrong. But sentiment has never figured in Lester's calculations and a trifling matter of family ties was not going to sway him here.

Naturally, Piggott's judgement was spot-on. Sweeping through from what seemed like an impossible position at the rear of the field, Sir Ivor exploded past Petingo in the shadow of the post, making Armstrong's colt look like a riding-school hack. Piggott's *sang-froid* was breathtaking, but it was nothing to the iceman's touch that he brought to Epsom a few weeks later.

Harry Wragg, champion jockey in 1941, whose penchant for leaving his challenge as late as possible earned him the nickname of The Head Waiter, said that the Derby was the easiest race in the world to ride in. Wragg, who won the Epsom Classic three times, explained that because everyone was so hyped up they did things they would normally never do, pushing and shoving and generally making a mess of what should have been treated as 'just another race', to use Lester's famous phrase after his first Derby win on Never Say Die. This was why Lester was so utterly out on his own in the Derby. He approached the most prestigious event in the Flat racing calendar as if it were the lowliest selling race at Pontefract. The fact that hundreds of thousands were out there on the Downs screaming their encouragement and millions more were watching on television worldwide left Lester totally unmoved.

Contemporaries who rode against him will tell you that while other jockeys betrayed their nerves with exaggerated chattering and joking in the weighing room before the race, Piggott would sit quietly in a corner, revealing no trace of emotion on that inscrutable face. It was the same on that nerve-jangling trek across the Downs to the start and then when the skittish colts were loaded one by one into the starting stalls. In the eerie silence that descends before the stalls burst open the only things a rider hears are the creaking of a saddle or the movement of the horse next to him. At that moment you could almost cut the tension with a knife, but Piggott would probably be projecting ahead to the certainty he had lined up for the 2.30 the following afternoon.

Bearing all that in mind, the manner of Sir Ivor's victory in the 1968 Derby still rates as one of the most stunning performances of Piggott's career and very possibly the greatest of them all. In terms of pure showmanship it has arguably never been surpassed.

After Sir Ivor's glittering Guineas triumph he became hot favourite for the Derby, but one anxiety persisted. On his breeding he was by no means certain to last the testing mile and a half. As the field stepped slowly around the parade ring, the muscular bay, his coat glinting like a seal's skin, looked in a different league to the rest in every way. But brilliant though he was, the niggling suspicion lingered that he just might not have the reserves to complement his blinding speed as they made that final climb to the winning post. The task for Piggott was to conserve that speed until the last possible moment. If there was a better man for the job O'Brien knew he had not been born, but even so Lester's late, late show on Sir Ivor left the Irishman and the rest of the watching world shaking their heads in disbelief.

Geoff Lewis is among several of Piggott's contemporaries who were lost in admiration for the way Piggott handled Sir Ivor that afternoon. 'That was the most confident race he ever rode and even by Lester's standards it was mind-boggling. I could not believe anyone could treat the Derby with such disdain,' Lewis says. Jimmy Lindley, another former colleague, analyses the achievement by saying: 'People always talk about Lester being the strongest finisher in the game and he was. But for me his biggest asset was his temperament and judgement throughout a race. He was so cool.'

Lindley was involved in one particular race, the Prix Kergorlay at Deauville in

Lester's greatest ride? Many saw it that way after he had produced Sir Ivor with an amazing late run to snatch the 1968 Derby from Connaught in the last 100 yards

1970, that illustrates how Piggott always out-thought and outmanoeuvered the rest as well as outriding them. Lindley was riding the Ascot Gold Cup winner Precipice Wood, with Piggott on O'Brien's colt Reindeer. Knowing that Precipice Wood was one of the bravest horses in training and would always pull out a little more when challenged, Piggott not only left his run incredibly late, he also deliberately launched his attack up the middle of the track away from his rival. When Reindeer burst ahead, the race was over and Precipice Wood had no time to respond.

There is almost always an x-factor in every race, the previously disappointing animal who decides that this is the day to run out of his skin and show the world exactly what he is made of. In the 1968 Derby that horse was the enigmatic giant Connaught, trained by Noel Murless and ridden by his new stable jockey, eighteen-year-old Sandy Barclay. The young Scotsman had replaced George Moore, who scuttled back to Australia after just one season because of threats made to him by big-time gamblers.

Murless knew Connaught was a good horse, but up to the Derby he was also a wickedly frustrating one. The brilliance of his work on the Heath in the mornings had never been fully reproduced on the racecourse and the problem was not helped by the fact that Connaught had an aversion to starting stalls.

As his chance of beating Sir Ivor looked negligible, Barclay decided to try something new with Connaught. He took the lead after only a quarter of a mile and allowed the big colt to bowl along in front. 'Connaught was loving it and when we turned into the straight still cantering I knew that whatever was behind me was going to have to be a bit special to beat me,' Barclay says. As Connaught struck for home, opening up a clear lead from his flagging rivals, Piggott appeared to be riding in a different horse race altogether. So casually was he ambling along behind the chasing group that it appeared he had must have had a brainstorm and ridden one of the worst-judged races of his life. With a furlong to run Lester had made some sort of forward move on Sir Ivor, but his chance of catching Connaught still looked non-existent. Suddenly he eased Sir Ivor to the outside and began to ride in earnest for the first time in the race. Even now he was not resorting to his whip, but nudging Sir Ivor along with hands and heels, showing no real sign of urgency.

O'Brien, who decribes Sir Ivor's Derby as among his all-time favourite memories of Piggott's riding, recalls: 'I watched the race with the late Bull Hancock who bought the horse as a yearling for Raymond Guest. With less than two furlongs to run Bull put his glasses down and said to me "He can't win now."' Guest must have turned greyer by the second as he watched his colt's agonising progress on a television set on a lawn in County Wexford. Guest, the American ambassador to Ireland, was attending the unveiling of the John F. Kennedy Memorial and as he breathlessly chanted 'Come on, Ivor! Come on, Ivor!' surrounded by a host of dignitaries there was more at stake than the sheer kudos of winning England's premier horse race. The previous summer, before Sir Ivor had shown the full extent of his potential, Guest had placed a bet of £500 each way on his colt for the Derby with William Hill at odds of 100–1. There is about as much chance of a bookie laying that sort of bet nowadays as there is of pigs winging over Epsom.

While Guest was going spare across the water, there was a collective gasp from the crowd as Piggott produced his spectacular final flourish. It was a denouement that racing folk would talk about for years. Sir Ivor came flying up on the outside, scuttled past Connaught with less than 100 yards to run and sped across the line with Piggott glancing across at the hapless Barclay as if to say: 'That's the way it's done, son.'

It was in fact a fatherly Piggott who comforted the tearful Barclay in the weighing room minutes later. Barclay, who is virtually out of racing these days apart from odd stints of work riding, found it impossible to believe that the greatest prize in Flat racing had been snatched from his grasp so cruelly. The memory still haunts him. 'I remember it as if it was yesterday. A furlong out there

RIGHT There's nothing to it: Lester tells commentator John Rickman how he makes riding the Epsom switchback seem easy (Gerry Cranham)

BELOW Piggott's fans can hardly believe their luck as he brings home Empery at odds of 10–1 to win the 1976 Derby (Gerry Cranham)

ABOVE Not for the first time Piggott holds the whip hand over Willie Carson as he drives The Minstrel ahead of Hot Grove to take the 1977 Derby. And (left) he is led back in triumph after a finish that many experts considered one of the strongest of his career (Gerry Cranham)

OPPOSITE Newmarket trains an eye on the ear of Piggott. Only a week before winning the 1981 1,000 Guineas on Fairy Footsteps, Lester had almost lost his ear in an horrific accident in the starting stalls at Epsom and the heavy bandaging is clearly visible as he returns to the winner's enclosure (Gerry Cranham)

ABOVE Record breaker: Piggott keeps Commanche Run going to land the 1984 St Leger and gain his twenty-eighth British Classic victory, beating Frank Buckle's record set 157 years earlier. And (right) he celebrates wearing the traditional St Leger cap (Gerry Cranham)

OPPOSITE Going solo: Lester is never seriously challenged as he coasts home on Teenoso to record his ninth and last Derby victory (Gerry Cranham)

LEFT Piggott canters to the start on the Queen's colt Milford before the 1979 Derby in which he finished unplaced behind Troy. And (below) he accepts Her Majesty's congratulations after winning the 1984 King George VI and Queen Elizabeth Diamond Stakes at Ascot on Teenoso (Gerry Cranham)

OPPOSITE TOP Piggott drives out Shadeed to win the 1985 2,000 Guineas and bring his British Classic tally to twenty-nine (Gerry Cranham)

OPPOSITE BELOW Lester's last winner, or is it? The racing world thought it was seeing the curtain come down on Piggott's riding career on the afternoon he brought home Full Choke to win at Nottingham in October 1985, but five years later he was back in the saddle (All-Sport)

Calm before the storm: Piggott leads his string out to exercise on Newmarket Heath during a training career cut short by his imprisonment (Gerry Cranham)

was no sign of anything and I thought I'd definitely won it,' Barclay says. 'By that time you can usually sense if something's going to come at you. Where Sir Ivor came from I just do not know. I felt he must have jumped in the race at the quarter-mile pole. Connaught wasn't stopping, but Sir Ivor absolutely flew past me.

'That look Lester gives you when he's going past is not a cheeky look. It's just a look of satisfaction at a job well done. He came up to me afterwards, put his hand on my shoulder and said: "Bad luck. There's plenty more Derbys. You'll get another chance."'

That touching little scene was in total contrast to the shenanigans at York the following year. Piggott and Barclay were involved in a desperately tight finish and it wasn't only Lester's mount that felt the sting of his whip, as Barclay explains.

'I was being held in on the rails by Lester and as we were battling it out he hit me across my back with his whip. I retaliated by hitting him with my whip and it ended up like a sword fight. We were hauled up before the stewards and before I could get a word in Lester said to them "Look at this." Then he lifted up his shirt and pointed to the weals on his back.

'I showed them my weals which were much worse and they eventually decided to disqualify Lester. He was none too pleased, I can tell you, and when we rode in the next race we had what you might call a heated contretemps. We didn't speak for some time after that, but eventually it was all forgotten and we ended up good buddies. Lester's far more sensitive that people imagine. He has feelings that run very deep.'

As for the year of Sir Ivor, that was only just beginning when he won the Derby. O'Brien ran him next in the Irish Derby where he was ridden by Liam Ward, who had an arrangement to ride the stable's horses in Ireland. Piggott rode Ribero, but felt he had as much chance of beating Sir Ivor as he had of being asked to become a member of the Jockey Club. All the way up the long, staring straight at the Curragh Piggott waited for Ward to come to him, but the Irishman never arrived. Ribero skated home by two lengths. Everyone seemed to blame poor Ward, but the finger should almost certainly have been pointed at Piggott. Once again the supreme Classic tactician had engineered a little masterpiece. Piggott knew Sir Ivor did not truly stay a mile and a half, therefore he set out to draw his sting. It was really simplicity itself – that is, if you had a racing brain with an inbuilt computer.

Sir Ivor's year went a little soft in the middle. A week after the Irish Derby, he was edged out by the four-year-olds, Royal Palace and Taj Dewan, in the Eclipse Stakes. After a summer holiday he finished second in a trial for Europe's most prestigious all-aged middle-distance event, the Prix de l'Arc de Triomphe, and in the Arc itself he was trounced by Vaguely Noble, a horse who was never given full credit for his brilliance. After that it was back to England for the Champion Stakes which he took in the style of the old, supercharged Sir Ivor. And finally there was drama, controversy and recrimination when Lester produced another Epsom-style surge to win the Washington International at Laurel.

There had been a heavy fall of snow before the Laurel event and Sir Ivor's chance of lasting the mile and a half in the boggy ground seemed painfully slim. Piggott etched a work of art in the Laurel mud, once again conserving Sir Ivor's afterburner thrust for the final 100 yards. There was a sticky moment rounding the final turn when Sir Ivor was momentarily up a blind alley, but it was only a minor irritation for Lester, who calmly popped him through a gap on the inside to win quite snugly in the end. Vintage Sir Ivor, vintage Piggott.

The hard-bitten American pressmen saw it differently, and laid into Piggott with rare venom. They were used to only one way of riding over there and that was to lie up close to the pace and go for the wire as soon as you could. Lester's display of legerdemain was an aberration as far as the US hacks were concerned and they let him know it. One went so far as to call him a 'limey bum'.

Piggott is remarkably philosophical about such attacks. He once explained his outlook thus: 'You learn to ride along with the praise and the criticism. I have won by a short head after making a hell of a mess of things and then read how brilliantly I rode. And when I have done everything right and just got caught on the post they have said I made a hash of things.' Looking back on the Laurel episode recently, he said: 'The press are entitled to their opinion. They were used to horses racing wide in those days and they thought that what I did was a bit out of order. But we were worried that he wouldn't get the trip in the ground and Vincent told me I had to hold him up as long as possible.'

Lester carries grudges with him for a long time, but he had only to wait twelve months before taking revenge in typically stinging fashion. Having ridden the same sort of race to take the Washington International again on Karabas, he was asked when he thought he had the race won. 'Two weeks ago!' he retorted. The mask momentarily dropped and a huge schoolboy grin broke out. In the next ten years or so, with O'Brien on song, Old Stoneface would by his standards be caught quite frequently with a smile on his face.

CHAPTER FOUR
THE BALLET DANCER AND
THE BASEBALL PLAYER

While Sir Ivor was carving himself pride of place in Lester's affections, a chunky little Canadian stallion named Northern Dancer was about to spark a breeding revolution that would send the O'Brien–Piggott Classic machine into orbit over the next decade.

Northern Dancer retired to stud in 1965 having won fourteen of his eighteen races, including two legs of the American Triple Crown, the Kentucky Derby and the Preakness Stakes. With this truck record it was only to be expected that he would entice a stream of breeders to his barn door, but no one could possibly have suspected that he would become the breeding phenomenon of the twentieth century. When Northern Dancer began covering mares his fee was $10,000. Twenty years later breeders were allegedly paying $1 million for his services, without even the guarantee of a foal.

When Northern Dancer was put down at the age of twenty-nine in November 1990 he had created an international dynasty of champions unmatched by any other Thoroughbred stallion in the modern era. Arab owners like the Maktoum family of Dubai bought their pre-eminence with the black gold of oil money, but the crimson gold flowing through Northern Dancer's veins was a currency that guaranteed him a far greater and more lasting place in the annals of horse racing. Not only did his progeny such as Nijinsky and The Minstrel – two of the four O'Brien–Piggott Derby winners – hammer home their supremacy on the racetracks; many of his sons have become potent sires in their own right, producing strings of champion offspring. And Northern Dancer's grandsons, such as Caerleon and Ile de Bourbon, are increasing his sphere of influence almost daily.

The Northern Dancer male line has produced seven winners of the Epsom Derby; in 1984 two of his sons, Secreto and El Gran Senor, finished first and second, separated by the width of a nostril. His bloodlines are dominant all over the world. Shortly after his death, Bernard McCormack, General Manager of Windfields Farm in Canada where Northern Dancer was born and buried, said: 'Very soon, if it has not happened already, more than 50 per cent of the world's Thoroughbred population will have Northern Dancer's blood in their pedigrees.'

Northern Dancer could be described as a freak of nature, yet in one respect this extraordinary founding father of modern racing was man-made. O'Brien's sixth sense told him that he had tapped into a vein of gold with Northern Dancer's progeny and he helped himself before others even realised the gilt-edged opportunities. One of those who did was Robert Sangster, whose partnership with O'Brien in the late seventies was responsible for sending Northern Dancer's stallion career into a heady orbit that changed the face of the bloodstock world. Sangster and O'Brien virtually cornered the market in Northern Dancer's progeny, making annual raids on the famous Keeneland Sales in Kentucky specifically to snap up that priceless blood. The Northern Dancer factor was largely responsible for sending bloodstock prices spiralling to previously unimagined levels. When Northern Dancer began his career the world record price for a yearling was $170,000. During the eighties, when the market reached its peak, one of his sons fetched $10.2 million and a grandson was sold for $13.1 million, figures that are now likely to be unsurpassed for some time.

The first of the Northern Dancer superhorses, Nijinsky, cost a mere $84,000 and was bought not by Sangster but Charles Engelhard, and not by conscious calculation but as a second choice! After his marvellous successes with Ribocco and Ribero, Engelhard was naturally keen to keep in with the Ribot family. He tried unsuccessfully to buy a half sister to those two colts at the Keeneland Sales in 1968, but was talked out of stepping over the $400,000 line by his racing manager, David McCall. Engelhard then dispatched his old friend O'Brien to Windfields Farm to take a look at a son of his favourite Italian stallion. O'Brien did not like the appearance of the Ribot colt, who had a rather suspect-looking leg, but he took an instant shine to a Northern Dancer colt and recommended him to Engelhard as an alternative. After getting the nod from his patron, O'Brien shelled out $84,000, a record sum in Canada, for the colt who turned out to be Northern Dancer's most famous son, Nijinsky.

The great Russian ballet dancer, Vaslaw Nijinsky, said on his deathbed that he would return to earth as a stallion. The four-legged Nijinsky certainly moved with an athleticism and grace that would not have disgraced the master of the entrechat, but his temperament was another matter altogether. At one stage during Nijinsky's early tutelage at Ballydoyle, O'Brien warned Engelhard that the colt might prove impossible to train. In his book *Vincent O'Brien's Great Horses*, Ivor Herbert recounts that the trainer sent a letter to Engelhard during the winter of 1968 telling him: 'I am somewhat concerned abut Nijinsky's temperament and that he is inclined to resent getting on with his work. My best boys are riding him and we can only hope that he will go the right way.' Vincent said subsequently: 'If I hadn't had first-class horsemen to ride Nijinsky I don't believe we would ever have succeeded with him. He could easily have gone the wrong way.'

Nijinsky would rear up, sweat up, sulk when he got to the gallops and generally refuse to cooperate. Piggott remembers that he was always looking at birds,

Piggott brings Nijinsky home ahead of the French colt, Gyr, to win the 1970 Derby and extend his unbeaten sequence to eight

anything rather than concentrate on the job in hand. But the whispering wizard O'Brien eventually got inside that handsome head and channelled the horse's fount of nervous energy in the right direction. The innate power that Vincent had sensed when he first glimpsed the relatively weak and immature Nijinsky picking at the grass at Windfields was eventually brought to full flower in a racing career that captured the imagination of professionals and public alike. The name of Nijinsky became a synonym for racetrack brilliance. When people use a yardstick to assess a present-day champion they tend not to compare him to Mill Reef or Sir Ivor or Dancing Brave. 'He's the new Nijinsky,' they will say.

Piggott did not get in on the act until the fifth and final race of Nijinsky's juvenile season. Liam Ward had ridden the strapping colt to authoritative victories in his four previous starts, but it was in the more rarefied atmosphere of Newmarket's Dewhurst Stakes that Nijinsky first sped across the racing firmament as a shooting star of exceptional brilliance. With Piggott at his most arrogantly confident, Nijinsky brushed aside the best of England's gilded youth to stamp himself as the outstanding Classics scholar of the class of '69.

Nijinsky's graduation the following spring was as smooth as it was inexorable.

The question 'Who will be second to Nijinsky?' posed by the *Sporting Life* on the morning of the 2,000 Guineas was answered with a sauntering solo run up the Rowley Mile. The Derby then appeared an equal formality, even though the French would not hear of defeat for their champion, Gyr.

In the event, it was not the Frenchman but the forces of nature that almost provided Nijinsky's downfall. A bout of colic, frequently an extremely serious affliction with horses, laid Nijinsky low the day before the Derby, after he had completed his final workout round the already buzzing Epsom circuit. Medication so close to the race would have been illegal, so the O'Brien team had to sweat it out along with the horse.

The crisis passed and as Derby day dawned under a searing June sun, it was the French connections who felt sick to the stomach. When Bill Williamson launched the white-faced Gyr into the lead early in the straight, the elegant colt looked like justifying all the arrogantly confident predictions that had been wafting across the Channel. But when Piggott unleashed Nijinsky it was all over within a few devastating strides. There was a moment when Nijinsky hung fire, but it had merely delayed the agony for the Gallic camp. 'He was running lazily two furlongs out and I had to get at him,' Piggott said. 'But in the end he did it like a good horse. Once he got in front he ran away.'

Through the summer the Nijinsky legend grew as that same flashing burst of acceleration brought him delectably executed wins in the Irish Derby (ridden by Ward) and King George VI and Queen Elizabeth Stakes to bring his unbeaten run to ten.

'Never use a superlative,' Joe Estes, the editor of the American publication *The Blood Horse*, once told a junior reporter. 'Nothing you run into on this kind of beat ever justifies a superlative.' Piggott and most of a bedazzled racing world were more than happy to ignore that dictum after Nijinsky had won the King George, although it was eventually to rebound on them with some force.

Nijinsky's opponents at Ascot comprised the previous year's Derby winner, Blakeney; the 1968 Italian Derby winner, Hogarth; the Washington International winner, Karabas; the French Oaks winner, Crepellana; and Caliban, winner of the Coronation Cup. For all their achievements, the quintet might as well have been rejects from the knacker's yard. When Piggott touched the accelerator pedal in the straight, Nijinsky eased past the others as if they had already been round the circuit twice. Hardly surprising, therefore, that after dismounting a beaming Piggott said: 'He is without doubt the greatest horse I have ever ridden.'

Engelhard then decided that Nijinsky would attempt to become the first horse since Bahram thirty-five years earlier to complete the Triple Crown of 2,000 Guineas, Derby and St Leger. It looked easy enough on paper, but nature intervened again, this time with far wider-reaching effects. Nijinsky duly cruised home from Meadowville in the St Leger to receive the plaudits of an ecstatic

ABOVE Easy does it: Piggott brings Nijinsky home on a tight rein to win the 1970 St Leger and become the first horse for thirty-five years to win the Triple Crown. And (right) he receives an unforgettable reception from the Doncaster crowd as he is led back

A stern-faced Piggott is accompanied back after being thrown from his mount at the start of St Leger day. People assumed the worst when they saw him hit the ground as there had been a threat to shoot him

crowd on Town Moor and bolster his claim to be the horse of the century, but all was not well with him.

Things had certainly not looked well for Lester when he was pitched off his opening mount of the afternoon. Not for the first time in his professional life, he had been the subject of a death threat. The police were informed that Piggott was going to be shot on Leger day and when he fell to earth before the start of the first race it seemed the worst had finally happened. Piggott, as usual, simply treated it all with detached amusement.

Nijinsky had been debilitated by a severe attack of ringworm before the St Leger and O'Brien had been forced to rush his preparation. This was undoubtedly a contributory factor in Nijinsky's first defeat, in the Prix de l'Arc de Triomphe at Longchamp in October. Even the French could not quite believe it when Yves Saint-Martin inched Sassafras home in front – and Piggott was immediately saddled with the blame.

Riding Nijinsky with sky-high confidence, Lester brought him from a long way back to head Sassafras in the straight, but in the dying strides Saint-Martin rallied his mount and got back in front again a few yards before the line. The head-on patrol film showed that Nijinsky had veered violently to his left in the final hundred yards, offering an instant explanation for the narrow loss, but O'Brien was said to be a very unhappy man. The diplomatic Vincent would be the last man openly to attack his jockey, but quite clearly he was not pleased at Piggott's exaggerated waiting tactics. Ironically, he had said beforehand: 'The Arc is a funny race and a hard one to win. It's better to be on the outside than the inside where you can get shut in. I expect him to lie up near the leaders as he could be the sort of horse who is difficult to extricate.'

Piggott's explanation of events was as follows: 'Things did not go right in the Arc. Nijinsky was really uptight that day. When we straightened up I had the option to go on the inside or the outside of two horses. I chose the outside to be on the safe side, which was probably a mistake. I headed Sassafras and I was going to beat him, but for some reason Nijinsky suddenly went left. I didn't have time to pull my whip through because we were right on top of the post, so instead of being a head in front I was a head behind.'

Nijinsky's swerve had been the deciding factor in the end. But Piggott had asked an awful lot of the horse and it has to be said that in relative terms this was not one of Lester's greatest rides. Three years later, Piggott won the Arc at his seventeenth attempt on Rheingold which puts one piece of xenophobic nonsense perpetuated by some British race fans into perspective: for while they have frequently pilloried the brilliant French jockey, Freddie Head, for his alleged inability to master the intricacies of Epsom, by comparison the relatively conventional Longchamp track should present no real problems for a top rider; yet it seemed to take Piggott some years to get fully to grips with the Parisian course.

A few weeks later it was O'Brien who made a tactical error when he sent Nijinsky to Newmarket for what was expected to be a triumphant curtain call in the Champion Stakes. In an unprecedented display of affection by the record crowd, Nijinsky was applauded down to the start. But by the end of the afternoon the legend had been irreparably tarnished. The traders trying to offload Nijinsky mementoes made a sorry sight after the sorrier one of Nijinsky being hammered into defeat by Lorenzaccio.

Nijinsky got himself in a terrible lather before the race and looking back both O'Brien and Piggott now realise that the Champion was a bridge too far. That was something that undoubtedly figured in Paul Cole's mind when he decided not to bring his dual Derby winner, Generous, back for the Champion after his failure in the 1991 Arc.

Piggott's retrospective assessment downgraded Nijinsky. 'The opposition to Nijinsky was not great. It was not a vintage year,' Piggott said. 'Overall I'd have to say Sir Ivor was the best. He ran on so many different tracks in so many different countries and he beat a lot of good horses.'

Between his King George and St Leger victories, Nijinsky was syndicated as a stallion for a world record $5.44 million. He joined Sir Ivor at Claiborne Farm in Kentucky as one of the elite band of equine Lotharios making a multi-million dollar industry out of nature. In the past two decades Nijinsky has gone a long way towards assuming the mantle of his illustrious father, Northern Dancer, producing champion progeny with amazing regularity. These included the wonderful Golden Fleece, also trained by O'Brien, who shattered the course record when winning the 1982 Derby and whose premature retirement denied him his proper place in racing's hall of fame.

No such problems for Lester. With five Derby successes in the bag, his place was already assured. There were still four more chapters to be added, however, and his triumphant Epsom progression led him from a ballet dancer to a baseball player. Just two years after Nijinsky, Lester rode Roberto – named after the Pittsburgh Pirates baseball star, Roberto Clemente – to what was one of the most brilliant but also the most controversial victory of his magnificent nine.

Shrugging aside any inhibiting thoughts of allegiance to O'Brien, Piggott had rejected Roberto after being beaten on him in France the previous year. Instead he committed himself for the 1972 Classics to the much-vaunted Crowned Prince, trained at Newmarket by Bernard Van Cutsem. Then, before he could take part in the 2,000 Guineas, Crowned Prince was found to have a soft palate and his career came to an abrupt end. Never a man to be embarrassed by such things, Lester would have nipped straight back in to resume the Roberto connection, had O'Brien not already signed up the Australian jockey Bill Williamson for the ride in both the Guineas and the Derby. After Roberto had run what appeared to be the perfect Derby trial in finishing a close second to the speedier High Top in the 2,000 Guineas, Piggott must have regretted his temporary desertion of the

O'Brien ship even more. Yet, as was so often the way of things, the wheel was turning inexorably in Lester's favour. What happened in the run-up to the Derby generated one of the most emotional and hotly debated incidents in the recent history of the sport.

With his permanently morose expression and immutably taciturn nature, Williamson would have justified the Old Stoneface tag every bit as much as Piggott. They nicknamed him 'Weary Willie' instead and despite his lack of rapport with the British public, Williamson carved himself a place in their affections, if only because it became obvious that the wily old Aussie was more than a bit useful in the saddle.

Behind the impenetrable mask old Bill was a bit of a wag. Jimmy Lindley recalls beating Williamson in a desperate finish to a lowly consolation plate at Windsor. 'After I had done Bill a short head he turned to me and said "Jeez, Jimmy. If I'd known you were that hard up I'd have given you a tenner."'

Piggott once said of Williamson: 'We never knew how old Bill was, but he was one of those people who always seemed old.' The Australian was in fact a relatively youthful forty-nine when he sat back and contemplated the very real prospect of finally achieving his greatest ambition – winning the Epsom Derby.

Fate moved in twelve days before Epsom when Williamson injured his shoulder in a fall at Kempton Park. By that time Piggott had accepted the mount on another O'Brien contender, Manitoulin, who carried the colours of Dorothy Galbreath, the wife of Roberto's owner, John. As a pleasurable diversion from his demanding business interests, the wealthy Galbreath had bought the Pittsburgh Pirates baseball team, who won the coveted World Series for him in the spring of 1972. When Galbreath flew over to London the weekend before the Derby and learned that Williamson had been injured, his instincts as a businessman and a sportsman set the red light flashing. Williamson assured Galbreath that he was fit to ride Roberto, but the 74-year-old American was unconvinced, even though Williamson was examined by the leading sports injury specialist, Bill Tucker, who pronounced the Australian in good shape. Galbreath had scented the unmatchable thrill of an English Derby victory and he was not going to be deprived of that unique honour by the avoidable error of an unfit jockey.

Galbreath knew a thing or two about sporting performance at the highest level and even if Williamson was 99.9 per cent fit that was not good enough. So he summoned the Australian to his suite at Claridge's two days before the Derby and told him that his services would not be required at Epsom; Lester Piggott would be aboard Roberto. Galbreath promised Williamson some £6,000 if Piggott rode Roberto to victory, equivalent to the percentage he would have picked up as the winning jockey. It was the American's idea of an acceptable sweetener, but as far as Williamson was concerned it had the sickening taste of bitter aloes.

The British public thought so, too. The news was greeted with unbridled hostility in the press and when Piggott brought Roberto back to the winner's

ABOVE Piggott edges Roberto (far side) ahead to win the 1972 Derby after a desperate struggle with Ernie Johnson on Rheingold. He was greeted in virtual silence, however, as feelings were running high over his last-minute substitution for the veteran Australian jockey, Bill Williamson (left)

enclosure after a victory that would normally have been hailed as a masterpiece of jockeyship, he was greeted with virtual silence. Williamson was welcomed like a conquering hero when he returned on two winners later in the afternoon.

The irony of the Roberto affair was that while on known form people would have been quite justified in assuming that Piggott was the villain of the piece, in this case he was innocent. There is only one Derby and apart from the prestige and the prize money, the winner instantly becomes worth a sheikh's ransom as a stallion. With his doubt about Williamson's fitness, Galbreath seized on the chance to employ the very best man for the job and that was Lester Piggott. It was as simple as that. But the racing world at large, not being aware of the full facts, believed that this was just another squalid example of Lester's practice of 'jocking off' colleagues, in other words, using his relationship with leading owners and trainers to snaffle a big-race ride at the expense of another jockey.

There is no doubt that whenever Lester saw the possibility of putting himself in line for a handsome pay cheque he would not hesitate to carry out some Machiavellian manoeuvering behind the scenes, shunting aside a contemporary without a thought. Howls of righteous indignation rang out regularly when he suddenly appeared on board a horse at the eleventh hour in place of the advertised jockey. This practice infuriated owners and trainers as well as the public, but they had to accept that this was Lester's modus operandi. When they wanted to be sure their horse was in the best hands they would seek him out before anyone else, but they were well aware that he could outfox the Scarlet Pimpernel.

Jeremy Tree, the Beckhampton trainer, for whom Piggott rode a host of big winners including the 1975 Oaks heroine, Juliette Marny, says: 'He was certainly not the most reliable person when it came to making arrangements. To be frank, you never knew whether Lester would definitely ride your horse until you saw him on it in the paddock before the race.' Still, being messed about by Piggott on occasions was a price that even the most illustrious professionals were usually willing to pay. Vincent O'Brien once said: 'The real charm of having Lester ride for you is that it gets him off the other fellow's horse.'

Whether Lester should be painted so black for what he did is a moot point. He knew he was the best jockey and he expected to ride the best horses. He built up a network of invaluable contacts over the years and he was entitled to make full use of them. Colleagues suffered by his actions, it is true, but racing is a business like any other and it is up to each individual to make his own way forward. Indeed, it is probably fair to say that most riders accepted it as a fact of professional life when they were substituted by Piggott and they did not hold it against him.

Clive Brittain defends Piggott by saying: 'Lester had every right to be loyal to himself. Riding the best horses is what excites him. If a better ride came along on the day of the race it never entered his mind that he couldn't make the switch and why shouldn't he?' And Geoff Lewis points out that Gordon Richards did almost exactly the same as Piggott when it came to engineering the best rides, only the personable Gordon was far more subtle about it. Lewis says: 'Gordon was the greatest manipulator of all time. How else did he manage to ride 269 winners in a season? The difference with Gordon was that he did it without hurting anyone's feelings.

'Lester was a businessman doing a businessman's job. It's a pity there aren't more English sportsmen with his attitude. It's no good being the best loser in the game. I remember being twenty in front of Lester in the championship one year, but after Frank Durr fell off and injured himself Lester snapped up fifteen of Frank's rides in a week. I could have done that, but I was too soft and it cost me the championship.'

The problem with Lester was the rather callous attitude he appeared to adopt. A perfect example was his record-breaking twenty-eighth Classic victory on Commanche Run in the 1984 St Leger. The American rider Darrel McHargue was stable jockey to Commanche Run's trainer, Luca Cumani, but Piggott was a personal friend of Ivan Allan, the colt's owner. Desperately keen to surpass Frank Buckle's record of twenty-seven Classic wins, Piggott telephoned Allan repeatedly at his Singapore home and eventually succeeded in talking himself on to Commanche Run's back. Once again the criticism was both widespread and vitriolic, but Piggott was oblivious to it all, as a much-chronicled little story illustrates.

McHargue did not travel to Doncaster, preferring to stay at home in Newmarket and play tennis. When the rain bucketed down on the morning of the race Lester was asked if it might spoil Commanche Run's chance. 'No,' Lester replied, 'but it might spoil Darrel McHargue's tennis!'

McHargue, incidentally, was unperturbed. 'If I were in Lester's position I'd have done exactly the same thing. I don't blame Lester, it's part of the business.'

After Lester had driven Commanche Run home by a neck in a tumultuous finish, the general consensus was that no one else could have won on the colt. The same had been said of Piggott's win on Roberto and it is worth recapping on that phenomenal ride to highlight another facet of Piggott's many-sided genius.

Tactical brilliance apart, Piggott was also way above the rest in terms of sheer strength. He is a very fit man with exceptional power for his size and he has the upper torso of a prize-fighter. On Roberto he was positively superhuman. When Roberto and Rheingold drew clear of the rest in the straight their pulsating nose-to-nose battle had an added dimension because Rheingold, ridden by Ernie Johnson, was hanging badly across Roberto, causing problems for Johnson and even more for Piggott.

That became clear, however, only when the head-on film was shown. What the watching world saw initially was Piggott laying into Roberto with a series of rapid-fire whip strokes that seemed to jerk O'Brien's colt forward as if he had been wired up to an electric current. Lester inched his nose in front right on the line and although no one could be certain as the judges pondered interminably over

Sheer physical strength was one of Piggott's greatest attributes and the source of his power can be glimpsed here in his athletic frame

the photograph, there was an air of inevitability about it. Somehow we knew that on occasions such as this Lester just does not get beaten. (Incidentally, those who thought Piggott's apparent flogging of Roberto was cruel would have been surprised at the verdict of the vet, who found the colt to be totally unmarked.)

To steal that vital inch or two Piggott used every trick in the book. In a tight finish he would force his mount's head down in the final stride. When it came to a decision that was 'on the nod' his horse's nose was often down flat while that of his rival's mount was up in the air, so he would edge the decision. Bruce Raymond recalls one extraordinary piece of Piggott piracy in the 1984 Italian Derby. 'Lester was riding Welnor and I was on Bob Back and he beat me a short head as usual. We were neck and neck for the last three furlongs. Then in the final couple of strides Lester gave his horse one whack on the head and one on the nose. Afterwards I asked him why he did it and he said "Its head was going up and that made it put its head down." It was incredible. How could he think of that in such a tight situation? No one else could do it.'

Piggott's account of the 1972 Derby reveals the problems he faced. 'Roberto was never going that well throughout the race. In the straight Rheingold was rolling into me even though Ernie Johnson was doing everything he could to keep him off. Roberto was not putting it all in so I had to really whack him and I didn't have much room to do it. I always felt that if I'd been beaten I'd have got the race anyway on a stewards' inquiry.'

Johnson, who had won the Derby three years earlier on Blakeney, concurs with Piggott's version of events and adds his own tribute. 'There is only a neck or half a length between a top jockey and a middle-order one, but that happens a lot in a season and Lester's incredible strength gives him that vital edge on more occasions than anyone else. If you use Lester at least you know you haven't got to beat him.

'When Lester is at his best like he was on Roberto he is the hardest jockey in the world to beat. He's certainly the best I've ever seen. He's right up there with the greats of sport like Muhammad Ali in boxing or George Best in football.'

During the seventies Piggott consolidated his status as an international sporting idol. Addicted to the Turf's most glittering and lucrative prizes, he pursued them across the globe with characteristic single-mindedness. His schedule would have been enough to finish off most normal human beings, but travel was something Piggott enjoyed for its own sake. He loved the cosmopolitan ambience of airports and the buzz he got from skipping from one meeting to another in planes and fast cars.

Piggott's routes to and from racecourses were often chosen to take in his favourite local ice cream and confectionery shops. Queues did not exist as far as he was concerned; indeed, nothing was allowed to stand in his path. Peter Richards, a wealthy racehorse owner and friend of Lester's, recounts a typical incident that occurred when Lester was hurrying from Goodwood to catch a plane to ride in France. 'We were negotiating the rush hour in London and Piggott ran into the back of another car. Without hesitation he leapt out, went up to the policeman who had arrived on the scene and said: "Look here, officer, I'm Lester Piggott and this man has just reversed into me." Without waiting for any reply, he jumped back in the car and sped off.'

When Piggott was riding for Robert Sangster he would regularly purloin Sangster's planes, helicopters and cars, leaving the millionaire owner fuming on the tarmac. 'Lester would tell my drivers and pilots, "Mr Sangster isn't coming, so you can take me instead." It eventually got so bad that I had to tell them to ignore what Lester said.

'I remember after Lester won the Irish Champion Stakes on Commanche Run,

Piggott enjoyed many top-level successes aboard the great French-trained filly, Dahlia, seen here winning the 1975 Benson and Hedges Gold Cup at York

his last ride in Ireland, he told my helicopter pilot that I would be another hour and disappeared in the helicopter himself. I had a house party of ten, including Larry Hagman, the actor, staying with me on the Isle of Man, and we were left stranded at the racetrack.'

Piggott's pursuit of excellence meant that he was unable to concentrate on maintaining his dominance in the numbers game. However, as long as he remained the number one choice for Europe's finest Thoroughbreds and his bank balance continued to swell, this did not much bother him. Having completed a run of eight consecutive titles when he took the jockeys' championship in 1971, he did not win it again until 1981, ceding the crown to Willie Carson (1972, 1973, 1978 and 1980), Pat Eddery (1974–7) and his old friend Joe Mercer, who finally achieved his lifetime's ambition by finishing top of the heap in 1979.

In 1975 Piggott's pre-eminence was granted official recognition with the award of an OBE. The following year he booted home Derby winner number seven, the French colt Empery, to beat the previous record of six wins jointly held by Steve Donoghue and Jem Robinson. The most extraordinary aspect of Empery's success was his starting price of 10–1. Much to their chagrin, punters had obviously listened to Lester's pre-race contention that it would take a shotgun to stop the 2,000 Guineas winner, Wollow.

Empery's trainer was the Paris-based Egyptian, Maurice Zilber, whose most memorable characteristic, apart from being a magician with difficult horses and a tartar with difficult owners, was the clacking noise produced by an ancient set of false teeth when he talked. Empery was owned by Nelson Bunker Hunt, an American oil and silver billionaire for whom Lester had ridden the great mare Dahlia to a host of prestigious victories in 1974 and 1975. Both horses were sired by Vaguely Noble, the horse who trounced Sir Ivor in the 1968 Prix de l'Arc de Triomphe. Empery's form might not have marked him down as a potential Derby winner, even with Piggott on his back, but in the race it was as if Lester were aboard another Nijinsky or Sir Ivor. Riding to the familiar pattern, he shot clear of Relkino to make the intricate business of winning the Derby once again seem as easy as a morning hack in the park.

In 1976, the year of Empery, Piggott also revived his association with Sir Noel Murless, easing home his final winner of the season for the Newmarket trainer at Lingfield in November. That brief rekindling of one of racing's most celebrated partnerships preceded a new, three-cornered liaison that lifted Lester's fortunes through the roof. If the seventies were the champagne years for Lester, 1977 was the best vintage of the lot.

CHAPTER FIVE
SANGSTER AND THE MONEY GAME

Money goes to money, they say, but that maxim had no place in the so-called 'glorious uncertainty' of racing until Robert Sangster set about turning the whole concept of racehorse ownership and breeding on its head.

Before Sangster broke the mould, owning racehorses had been largely an exercise in ego-inflation for the very rich. Having one's colours carried on the back of a sleek and pricey Thoroughbred was another facet of the status-symbol culture, complementing the limousine and the yacht. At the other end of the scale, there were also those with less money who, through the ownership or part-ownership of a cheaply bought horse, or an involvement in breeding in a small way, enjoyed being part of the heady ambience of the sport of kings, even at the lowliest level. What the little fish had in common with the very rich was that neither expected to make money out of their pastime. They were in it purely for 'the crack'.

Sangster's early dalliance with the Turf was purely a fun thing. Owning a few racehorses offered a natural and pleasant social diversion for the dashing young man who was heir to Vernon Sangster, head of the Vernons pools empire. Having enjoyed considerable success with his early horses and landed a few notable gambles as well, he became fascinated by the business of breeding. He purchased the Swettenham Stud in Cheshire, thereby sowing the seeds of a totally new approach to racing and breeding that was to change the face of the sport during the seventies and eighties. Sangster was to become leading owner on the British Turf in 1977, 1978, 1982, 1983 and 1984. His dominance of the domestic scene was similar to that achieved by the Aga Khan in the pre-war era, but it was ended summarily by the arrival of the Maktoum brothers of Dubai, whose vast spending power relegated Sangster to the role of impotent onlooker at the major bloodstock sales.

Ironically, it was problems with his inheritance of the pools firm that nudged Sangster into a more serious involvement with racing. 'I inherited a third of Vernons shares when I was thirty and another third when I was thirty-five. I had to pay substantial capital gains tax on both occasions and I had to borrow money in order to do so,' he explains. 'When I was thirty-eight Vernons was due to go public, with me retaining twenty per cent of the company. The day before the launch Ted Heath called a general election. Labour came in, the stock market plunged and the market value of Vernons dropped dramatically. So when I became forty and inherited the last third I could have been technically bankrupt and yet still owned the company.

'I tried for a quick sale of the company and negotiated unsuccessfully with Lord White of the Hanson Trust, who wanted to carry out a sort of asset-stripping operation, keeping the football pools operation and selling off the subsidiary businesses. I also talked to Charles Clore of Sears Holdings and the Rank Organisation [he subsequently sold out to Thomson T-Line for £90 million in 1987 and resigned from the board of Thomson when they in turn were taken over by the bookmaking firm Ladbrokes]. In the end I was forced to move out of the country before my fortieth birthday to avoid the capital gains tax that would have been due.

'At that time the top rate of income tax was 98 per cent under Harold Wilson's Labour government. I had been working long hours at Vernons anyway, so I decided to take a year off and went to live in Marbella. After six months I decided I couldn't just spend my life playing golf five days a week. It was then that I decided to move to the Isle of Man and hit on the idea of making a business out of stallion syndication.'

Sangster already knew Vincent O'Brien and his son-in-law, John Magnier, the young genius of the Irish breeding scene. He wanted only the very best for his new business venture and decided that as these two men were the acknowledged masters of their respective fields they were the ones he must have as partners. In 1975 the trio jetted over to the internationally renowned Keeneland Sales in Kentucky with money to burn. The idea was to use O'Brien's expertise in picking out prospective champions, train them to win Classic races and syndicate them for vast sums as stallions at their Coolmore Stud complex close to O'Brien's Ballydoyle yard.

Sangster and Magnier had made their first venture into the syndication business four years earlier when they purchased Green God and Deep Diver from David Robinson to stand as stallions. Robinson, the television and radio rentals tycoon, had preceded Sangster in adopting a businessman's approach to his racing, but he had not delved into the far more lucrative stallion business.

Sangster will admit, incidentally, that even with his carefully calculated approach he owes a slice of his pre-eminence to luck. He once said that life is all about timing, and perhaps that should be broadened to encompass being in the right place at the right time – or having someone else there on your behalf. A classic example was his purchase of the French and Irish Derby winner, Assert. The day after Sangster won the Prix de l'Arc de Triomphe with Detroit (ridden by Pat Eddery), he had organised a celebration lunch at the Georges V Hotel in Paris. Pat Hogan, the well-known Irish bloodstock agent and a long-time friend and associate of Sangster, told him that he had seen a yearling he thought Sangster should buy which was due to come up at the Arc sale that afternoon.

According to Sangster, Hogan conforms to the music-hall image of his nationality in that he is not blessed with the greatest intellect. 'He used to write "Georges Sank" on his luggage labels,' Sangster laughs. However, Sangster readily confirms that Hogan is almost in the O'Brien class when it comes to picking out high-class young horses. 'Pat was responsible for buying the Arc winner, Detroit, for me. He had selected her when she was a foal with Roland de Chambure. She was in a field in Normandy with some of my foals and I bought her for about £100,000 from de Chambure and Alec Head.

'Anyway, the day after the Arc, Pat asked me how much I would go to for this yearling that he had seen at the Arc sale and I gave him a limit of £50,000. He was worried about missing the plane back, but managed to stay on and buy the horse for 160,000 francs [about £16,000]. The colt turned out to be Assert and we syndicated him for $25 million at the end of his three-year-old career.'

Even Sangster could not possibly have envisaged that sort of jackpot when he and his partners made that first strike on Keeneland. They spent over $1 million on a dozen choice yearlings, with Northern Dancer blood the cornerstone of their buying operation, as it would be for many years to come. That left them with one last element to add to the equation. And when it came to choosing a rider to handle those valuable equine commodities on the racetrack there was only one candidate on their short-list – the ultimate Classic pilot, Lester Piggott.

Piggott's contract with Sangster, which ran from 1977 to 1980, elevated him from being merely wealthy into the league of the super-rich. This happened largely through the long-established practice of owners giving valuable 'presents' to leading riders, on top of their riding fees and official retainers. These presents were usually in the form of cash or shares in stallions they had ridden. When the Sangster operation sent bloodstock prices spiralling the presents perk became a whole new golden ballgame. Piggott was virtually handed a licence to print money as the horses he rode for Sangster were syndicated for millions of dollars. Sadly, however, in one way the vast inflow of wealth was to act like a pair of golden handcuffs and a few years later it all came crashing down around Lester's ears.

At the beginning of 1977 the Sangster master-plan appeared to be proceeding remarkably smoothly. The horses bought at Keeneland two years previously were now at the crucial three-year-old stage of their careers and among the clutch of potential champions two in particular stood out as the preparatory work for the new Flat season began in earnest at Ballydoyle. These two Sangster standard-bearers were a flashy chestnut son of Northern Dancer named The Minstrel and the filly Cloonlara, a daughter of Sir Ivor. Each had won all three of its juvenile starts in a manner that suggested they had only to maintain their brilliance from two years to three for the English Classics to be theirs for the taking. However, as the spring of 1977 ebbed away that simple presumption turned into a nightmare.

85

After a less than impressive reappearance at Ascot, The Minstrel was beaten into third place in the 2,000 Guineas, two lengths behind Nebbiolo. Then, when he was inched out by Pampapaul in the Irish Guineas, it seemed he might well have been overrated. What is more, Piggott had been forced to give The Minstrel three hard races in succession, so the colt's prospects of redeeming himself in the Derby did not appear at all bright.

Before The Minstrel ran in the Guineas, Lester travelled over to Ballydoyle to ride the colt in a gallop, which led to a memorable contretemps between him and O'Brien. Piggott might be regarded as the supreme race rider, but when it comes to riding work he is seen as nothing short of a menace. When Lester arrives to put a horse through its paces in the cold light of dawn, trainers' instructions, aimed at providing a measured preparation, are totally ignored. All he is interested in is belting along as fast as possible and if anything goes past him during the workout that is the one he wants to ride.

So it was at Ballydoyle that chilly April morning when Lester went out on The Minstrel to work seven and a half furlongs in company with Artaius and Be My Guest, who were to prove themselves outstanding milers later in the season. O'Brien's instructions were that the three should stay together in a line, but as the other two made their way up the hill from the starting point known as The Bounds, there was no sign of Lester. Suddenly Piggott gave The Minstrel two backhanders and he came flying up on the outside. He went past the other two as if they were rooted to the spot and finished two lengths ahead of them. The gallop had been designed to bring The Minstrel on steadily with the Classics in mind, but the colt walked back blowing like a Chelsea Pensioner. Piggott commented nonchalantly: 'Something must have frightened him out there' and added 'He isn't half going well.'

O'Brien's face was as black as the storm clouds scudding across the early-morning Tipperary sky. He jumped down off the little rostrum from which he always watched the gallops and stormed back into the house without saying a word to anyone. The Whispering Doctor might come across in public as a mild-mannered introvert who would never raise his voice to anyone, but back in his own domain it is very different. O'Brien is in every sense master of Ballydoyle's 500 acres of rolling Irish countryside. He is a perfectionist and a stickler for detail and God help anyone if there is a hair out of place on one of those immensely valuable Thoroughbreds. Inside Ballydoyle he is known openly as 'The Führer'. 'When Vincent comes down into the yard in the morning, fifty people go flying,' his wife Jacqueline told me.

To say O'Brien was furious with Piggott for messing up the carefully planned gallop would be a major understatement. Piggott was banned from riding work at Ballydoyle for a month and when he returned O'Brien got his own back with interest. He handed Piggott a list of ten backward two-year-olds and told him that he wanted Lester to work each one over four furlongs up the sawdust gallop and provide detailed reports on all of them. It was a particularly filthy morning, with the rain sheeting in horizontally. But to give Lester his due, he never complained and rode them all as instructed. O'Brien had won another psychological battle, though, because Piggott did not come back to ride work at Ballydoyle again that year.

After The Minstrel's two Guineas defeats Ballydoyle was not a bright and happy place to be anyway. One by one the embryo champions were failing to deliver and the media were suggesting that the slump heralded the end for O'Brien. Even Sangster was sunk in gloom and he remembers seriously questioning the wisdom of his new venture. 'The Minstrel and Cloonlara had let us down badly and we hadn't got a Classic winner under our belt. What is more we had spent serious money buying more yearlings at Keeneland the previous year. I was thinking, Jesus, is this a good game to be in or not?'

'I couldn't have been lower after The Minstrel was beaten at the Curragh and then Lester sent me a message that I was to come and see him in the weighing room. I'll never forget the scene in there, it was like a disused railway station. There were empty champagne bottles lying all around (champagne is traditionally distributed by the winning rider) and Lester was sitting there in his string vest.

'He said to me in that offhand way of his, "If you run The Minstrel in the Derby, I'll ride him." When Lester speaks you pay attention or you make a big mistake, so I knew that The Minstrel would go to Epsom with a decent chance.'

Piggott had in fact been trying to get the ride on the Aga Khan's unbeaten French colt, Blushing Groom, but the Aga stayed loyal to his French jockey, Henri Samani. In that context, Piggott clearly did not rate The Minstrel's chance at Epsom so very highly. Indeed, punters would have backed anything but The Minstrel had they been able to tune in to Lester's pre-race thoughts.

John Gosden, now training probably England's largest string of horses for Sheikh Mohammed at Newmarket, was then assistant to O'Brien and led The Minstrel up at Epsom. He recalls the events of Derby Day 1977 vividly. 'Ballydoyle was in a slump and Lester was going through a real crisis of confidence. Before the race he was coming out with things like "Some of those pricks are saying I've gone, but it's you guys. You can't get the horses right." He was also convinced that Blushing Groom would win easily.

'The Minstrel was very highly strung, so we put cotton wool in his ears to blot out the noise of the crowds. I led him down to the start and I remember the gypsies were calling out things like "Go for it, Lester" and "Give him a good whipping, Lester" and for once Lester was getting really wound up. At one point he turned round and said "I don't know what I'm riding this f—g horse for."'

A few minutes later Piggott's demeanour had improved beyond measure after he had ridden The Minstrel to win by a neck from Hot Grove. 'King Lester VIII' the headline in the London *Evening Standard* read, and Piggott's handling of The Minstrel fully justified that label. 'The Minstrel's victories in the Derby and King

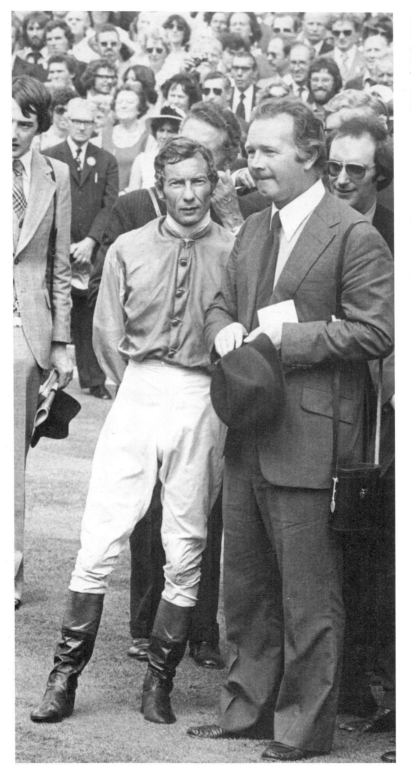

LEFT Royal command: Piggott and Robert Sangster await their presentation to the Queen after the victory of The Minstrel in the 1977 King George VI and Queen Elizabeth Stakes at Ascot

OPPOSITE TOP Piggott brings Alleged home to win the 1977 Prix de l'Arc de Triomphe. The combination won the race again the following year. Piggott was not always seen at his best in the Arc, however, and here (opposite, below) he fails narrowly on Ardross (black and white colours) in the 1982 running which Charles St George, the owner, felt he should have won

George VI and Queen Elizabeth Stakes were for me among the most memorable pieces of riding of Lester's career,' O'Brien says. 'Had he not been riding, I doubt if the horse would have won.'

When Willie Carson poached a long lead on Hot Grove early in the straight at Epsom, The Minstrel was already under strong pressure, but Piggott locked himself into one of those finishes that seem irresistible. Carson is himself one of the hardest men to beat in a tight contest, but as he threw in everything to try to keep The Minstrel at bay, Lester surged inexorably closer and edged in front yards from the line. Many experts echoed O'Brien's opinion that no one else in the world could have got The Minstrel home in front that day.

Gosden had been watching some way from the finishing post and rushed up to Piggott just as he was pulling up. 'I said to him "How did you do, Lester?" and he just answered "F—k off!"'

Suddenly the roller-coaster of racing fortune lifted Sangster and his team from the depths to a dizzy high. The Minstrel went on to win the Irish Derby and the King George before being retired to stud back at Windfields Farm. Eddie Taylor, his breeder, paid $4.5 million for a half share, valuing The Minstrel at $9 million. Not, after all, such a bad piece of business by Sangster, who had originally paid $200,000 for the colt.

Among a host of prestigious winners that year, Sangster also had the champion sprinter in Godswalk and the champion two-year-old, Try My Best, although the latter was to prove an inglorious failure the following year. But the best was saved until last with the magnificent triumph of Alleged in the Prix de l'Arc de Triomphe.

After winning his first five races, Alleged was thought to be unbeatable in the St Leger, but the Oaks winner, Dunfermline, wore him down to win by half a length. Sangster says that he regards that as the only bad race Piggott ever rode for him. 'Lester was told to hold Alleged up, but he kicked on early in the straight and acted like a pacemaker for Willie Carson on Dunfermline. Vincent was so devastated he dropped his binoculars before the finish.'

Piggott certainly made amends in the Arc, although ironically he disregarded O'Brien's instructions again in doing so. Having finally won the race on Rheingold four years earlier had helped to erase the nagging memory of Nijinsky's narrow defeat and, handling Alleged with maximum *élan* and confidence, he rode the French jockeys to sleep. Slipping into the lead after three furlongs, Lester kicked, slowed the pace and then kicked again, totally bamboozling the opposition to win comfortably from Balmerino.

Alleged returned to win the Arc again twelve months later, with Piggott easing him home two lengths ahead of Trillion. Alleged was retired with earnings of over £327,000 in win prize money, a record for a horse trained in Britain or Ireland. He had been bought for $175,000 and his stud value was set at $16 million, making him the most valuable horse in European racing history.

Stallions are usually syndicated on the basis of forty shares. During the eighties single shares in Nijinsky, Roberto, The Minstrel and Alleged changed hands for six- and even seven-figure sums, so given those sort of highly acceptable little 'presents' it was no wonder that Piggott's cash flow became a flood.

Piggott and Sangster were not feeling quite so flush after the Joe McGrath Memorial Stakes at Leopardstown in 1978. Barry Hills, one of Sangster's English trainers and a long-standing friend, asked Sangster if he could have Piggott to ride his good three-year-old, Sexton Blake. Sangster said yes, but two days before the race O'Brien decided to run Sangster's colt, Inkerman. Lester was claimed to ride Inkerman and Ernie Johnson took over on Sexton Blake. 'Lester told me that Inkerman had no chance of beating Sexton Blake. So I said in that case let's have a thumping great bet on Sexton Blake,' Sangster recalls. 'In the race Lester was sailing along in the lead looking over his shoulder to see where Sexton Blake was. But Ernie Johnson had given his horse far too much to do and Lester won easily.

'As we were going down the escalator I heard someone behind us saying "That Hills and Sangster, they're a pair of bloody crooks. They fixed the race." Little did they know that our money had gone down the pan with theirs.'

That episode was undoubtedly instrumental in Hills's decision to look for another stable jockey the following year, and that was when Sangster brought over the American prodigy, Steve Cauthen, to ride for himself and Hills. Cauthen had won over $6 million and ridden 487 winners from 2,075 rides in 1977 when he was only seventeen and the following year he won the American Triple Crown on Affirmed – but suddenly it all went wrong. Sangster was quick to take his opportunity.

'I was in Barbados and I picked up a copy of *Time* magazine and saw the headline "Superbug hits bad patch" ['bug' is the American word for an apprentice]. Steve had hit a losing streak of sixty at Santa Anita and I asked Billy McDonald [Sangster's friend and a well-known bloodstock wheeler dealer], who was in the States trying to buy the dam of Spectacular Bid for me, to ask Steve if he would be interested in a job in England. Then I flew out to sign him up.' In 1984 Cauthen became to first American to win the British jockeys' championship since Danny Maher in 1908.

Piggott continued to clock up big winners for Sangster during the remainder of their liaison, but there were no more English Classic successes, only two in Ireland. These were the 1978 Irish 2,000 Guineas, with Jaazeiro, and the 1979 Irish 1,000 Guineas, with Godetia.

On the subject of fillies, Piggott was given a rough time by two of Sangster's finest, Durtal and Cloonlara. Piggott suffered many horrendous falls during his career, but none was as potentially lethal as the episode involving Durtal before the 1977 Oaks, for which she started a hot favourite.

Durtal was very edgy before the race and on the way to the start she ran into a rail and Lester broke his stirrup iron. The filly then took off and tried to jump

Horrific falls were a feature of Piggott's career and he was frequently lucky to escape serious injury. Here (above) he is carried from the course after a fall at Lincoln as a fifteen-year-old and (left) he is about to be unshipped and dragged along by Durtal before the start of the 1977 Oaks

another running rail, spiking herself in the process. Piggott had his foot caught in his other stirrup and was dragged along. He might easily have been maimed or even killed, but typically he dusted himself off and rode in the last two races on the card, winning the final event with a nonchalance that suggested he had enjoyed a fairly uneventful afternoon.

Lester showed almost equal stoicism when he rode Cloonlara in the Prix de la Porte Maillot at Longchamp the day after The Minstrel won the Irish Derby. Cloonlara had been a brilliant two-year-old but had fallen out of love with the game and the French race was her last race before she was retired to stud. John Gosden, who travelled over with Cloonlara, describes the events of that fraught afternoon in Paris. 'After Cloonlara had been installed she suddenly flipped over backwards and broke her stall. Lester was dumped on the ground and only just got out of her way in time.

'He went to jump back on board, but the French stalls handlers shouted "Non, Monsieur. C'est impossible." Lester ignored them and led Cloonlara into another stall. Then he climbed up on the other stall like a monkey and dropped down on her back, ignoring the French protests. In the end he improved her draw position, but she was well beaten.'

Piggott's courage in such situations has always been well recognised, but his obsession with always getting back into the saddle as soon as possible was born out of something more than mere bravery. He was desperately worried that if he missed a mount he might forfeit the right to ride that horse and possibly others in the future. And losing potential winners was something that did not please Lester at all.

As the seventies ebbed away, Piggott's relationship with Sangster and O'Brien became increasingly strained. Despite his love of travelling, Piggott was said to be growing weary of the continuous toing and froing to Ireland, but Sangster says that there were lots of little things that led to the eventual break-up in 1980. Once again, there was no doubt that Piggott's desire to have the best of all worlds played a major part in the deterioration of the relationship. Piggott wanted to be allowed a free rein and yet keep the Sangster arrangement intact, but even the easy-going Sangster's tolerance had its limit.

One thing that particularly stuck in Sangster's craw was Piggott's bad-mouthing of Monteverdi, the champion two-year-old of 1979. Monteverdi had looked another super colt in the mould of The Minstrel after winning his four races as a juvenile, but he failed to reproduce the magic the following year. After Monteverdi finished unplaced in the Irish 2,000 Guineas a stern-faced Piggott jumped down from his back and dismissed him as a non-entity. A prospective stallion's career is carefully promoted to make him as attractive as possible to breeders at the end of his racing days and one wrong word can easily knock a nought or two off his value. It was hardly surprising, therefore that Sangster and his associates were not best pleased with Piggott's insult.

Another episode that hastened the end of the partnership concerned Sangster's runner in the 1980 King George VI and Queen Elizabeth Stakes, Gregorian, although in this case Piggott's non-cooperation did not prevent Sangster from obtaining an unexpected windfall.

The late-developing Gregorian did not show his true merit until he was a four-year-old. O'Brien sent him over to win the Westbury Stakes and the Brigadier Gerard Stakes at Sandown in the spring and he returned to the course to finish a good third behind Ela-Mana-Mou in the prestigious Eclipse Stakes, which Piggott looked to have stolen at one point with a dashing piece of opportunism that almost caught the rest unawares.

Piggott's riding of Gregorian when the horse finished third to My Hollow in the Royal Whip at the Curragh later that month was contrastingly disappointing, as Sangster explains. 'We knew that Lester was keen to ride the Prix de Diane winner, Mrs Penny, in the King George VI and Queen Elizabeth Stakes at Ascot the following week and frankly he did not produce one of his most inspired rides on Gregorian at the Curragh.

'I was still keen to run Gregorian at Ascot, even though Vincent was not. We had been to Keeneland Sales that week and flew back on Concorde to London. We had time to kill before our connecting flight and I went drinking in Harry's Bar with Vincent's brother, Phonsie, and John Magnier. Vincent had been teetotal for about three years and as he didn't want to come with us I told my driver to take him round the countryside before we met up at Gatwick for our ongoing flight.

'We were drinking Bellinis [a mixture of champagne and peach juice] and when we left Harry's Bar we took some little bags of Bellinis with us and gave them to Vincent, telling him that they were just peach juice. After Vincent had consumed a few of those and mellowed considerably it was no problem convincing him to change his mind and run Gregorian in the King George. Vincent doesn't know to this day that there was champagne in those "peach juices".'

Tommy Murphy took over on Gregorian at Ascot and although he did not get past Lester on Mrs Penny, he finished a creditable third. Sangster must have enjoyed a fair degree of schadenfreude watching Piggott's best-laid plans being thwarted when Mrs Penny found Ela-Mana-Mou threequarters of a length too good for her at the finish.

There was another reason why the Bollinger was flowing when Sangster returned to the Isle of Man. 'Those few bags of Bellinis earned me £2 million,' Sangster recalls with amusement, referring to the fact that Gregorian's third place in the Ascot race made him a far more valuable stallion prospect than he would otherwise have been.

Piggott's switch to Mrs Penny had renewed speculation that Sangster was intent on replacing him with Pat Eddery, who had already won the jockeys' championship four times. Media pressure forced Sangster to reveal his hand the day before the King George. 'I had heard Pat was unhappy with his position at Peter Walwyn's yard and I approached him a few weeks before the King George and told him that if he was dissatisfied he should consider leaving to ride for us. The day before the Ascot race Walwyn went into the press room and announced "The IRA have stolen my jockey." Later that afternoon when I was watching the Test match at home I received about twenty phone calls from the press asking if it was true that I had lined Pat up to replace Lester and I had to admit that I had approached him.'

Sangster was not the first man to have been pushed too far by Piggott's blatant opportunism and he would not be the last. However, Sangster is too much of a diplomat to make a public condemnation of such behaviour and he was subsequently subjected to an extremely awkward moment when he appeared on television in Australia, during an interview by the veteran Australian sports writer, Jack Elliott, on his *World of Sport* programme.

'I said to Jack before the show, "None of this patsy stuff, be hard on me. It makes a better show." Even so I was knocked back when he went straight in and asked me, "Did you sack Lester Piggott or did he sack you?" I had not had much

Piggott with champion trainer Henry Cecil (centre) and owner Charles St George, for whom he rode many top-class horses

sleep that night and it was the last thing I needed at eight o'clock in the morning. I just said the arrangement hadn't been working and skirted round it.'

When Sangster signed Eddery up for the following season it precipitated a remarkable chain reaction, the centrepiece of which was Walwyn's surprise signing of Joe Mercer as a replacement for Eddery. Mercer had appeared settled in his position as first jockey to Henry Cecil, who had carried on the tradition of excellence begun by his father-in-law, Sir Noel Murless, at Warren Place. Mercer had joined Cecil three years earlier and won his first jockeys' title in 1979, but now announced that the pressure of riding for a yard in Newmarket when his home was in Berkshire had begun to take its toll.

The dashing Cecil had topped the trainers' table three times and was well established as the dominant figure of his profession in every sense. With his elegance, good looks and theatrical manner allied to his wealth and position, Cecil is always news both on and off the racecourse. Whether he is winding up a post-race press conference with a wave of his hand and a cry of 'Cut!' or supervising early-morning gallops on Newmarket Heath from the back of his white Arab hack, dressed in chaps and cowboy boots with purple tassels, his flamboyance and assurance mark him out as the centre of attention. For Cecil suddenly to find himself without a stable jockey was rather like Liz Taylor being strapped for a husband, but the embarrassment predictably did not last for long. Within days of Mercer high-tailing it back to Berkshire, Piggott had swooped.

When Eddery moved into the Ballydoyle hot seat the cynics had been only too quick to kill off Piggott's career once again. Out on his ear without a major contract – even Lester won't recover from this, they said. Certainly, Piggott might have appeared crazy to kiss off the Sangster link. The scale of Sangster's operation at that time was daunting. He owned or partly owned 279 horses in training with thirty-six trainers in six different countries. His equine empire was completed by a fabulous collection of stallions, mares, yearlings and foals numbering over 400 in all. Piggott's greed had enabled Eddery to move in for the crock of gold that could still have been his, but he wasn't crying too much. He was back at Warren Place, where the legend had first taken flight a quarter of a century previously.

CHAPTER SIX
ALL GOOD THINGS MUST END

Anyone who signed up Lester Piggott knew they were in for a bumpy ride. Like an incurable philanderer who can never be faithful to one woman, Piggott's wandering eyes made it impossible to tie him down totally, even if the arrangement was formalised.

In one sense, therefore, Cecil was making a rod for his own back when he rubber-stamped Lester's return to the big house on the hill. The gliterati of the racing world who sent their horses to Warren Place expected nothing less than five-star treatment and that did not include being messed about by the stable jockey. One of those patrons, Daniel Wildenstein, eventually made a very public stand over Piggott's antics, as will be described later in this chapter. At forty-five, too, Piggott was no spring chicken and if Cecil had taken a long-term view he might have plumped for a younger rider. But any such negative aspects were easily forgotten when offset against the positive. Piggott's genius burned as brightly as ever; he was still the rider most capable of conjuring that hidden extra from his mounts. Even with men like Eddery, Carson and Cauthen around, owners and trainers immediately homed in on Piggott when it came to the high-profile occasion.

Sitting in his study at Warren Place, Cecil comes across as far quieter and more relaxed than the effusive, highly-strung individual the public has come to know. The champagne and Gucci image had been replaced by jeans, a can of lager and a packet of fags as he briefly explained some of the reasons why he jumped in to sign Lester and why he still rates him the best.

'Basically, Lester has always been the total professional. He would tell you such important things about your horses, but what made him invaluable as a stable jockey was that during a race he was always looking at the other horses around him and therefore he invariably knew the strength of the opposition. That was why he was never a person you would want riding against you.

'He was a terrible man to give orders to and eventually I never bothered, but contrary to what others have said I found him very professional when it came to riding work. Overall we had an excellent working relationship and a very good personal one as well. I found him a very thoughtful and kind person. For

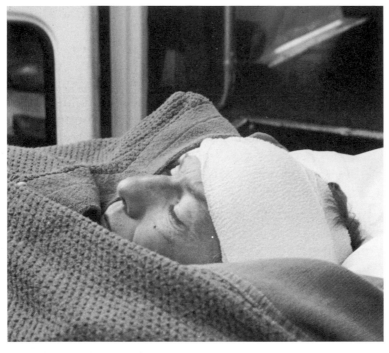

Piggott is in extreme pain as he is loaded into the ambulance after an accident in the starting stalls at Epsom. His ear was almost severed and he badly damaged his back, but he returned in time to ride Fairy Footsteps (below) to victory in the 1,000 Guineas a week later

example, when I was in hospital for an ulcer operation he was always on the phone making sure that Julie was all right and offering help.'

The new partnership struck oil straight away with the success of Fairy Footsteps in the 1981 1,000 Guineas. But just a week before Lester had urged the filly to victory at Newmarket, he had been down and out and looking unlikely to ride anything for a very long time. Television viewers tuned in to the Epsom spring meeting watched in horror as Winsor Boy dived under the bottom of the starting stalls and somehow scrambled underneath the metal superstructure like an equine limbo dancer, dragging Lester with him. As Piggott was stretchered away swathed in bandages all you could see of him was his eyes and nose, but the appalling pain was all too evident.

Piggott's right ear was almost severed and had to be sewn back on by a plastic surgeon at Roehampton Hospital. Susan Piggott bought a red, white and blue woollen headband of the sort usually worn by skiers and Lester wore it over his ear when he dragged himself back into action at Ascot a mere six days later. That headband is now among the Piggott memorabilia at the National Horseracing Museum in Newmarket.

The pain from the car injury was nothing compared to the agony from Lester's back, which had been scraped against the underside of the starting gate and was severely bruised and battered. Julie Cecil has the highest admiration not only for the way Lester made it back into the saddle so soon, but also for the stoicism that he displayed to win on Fairy Footsteps. 'Lester never squeals about anything. He takes whatever life throws at him and just gets on with it,' Julie says. 'What he went through to win on Fairy Footsteps was incredible. All the publicity was about his ear and people didn't realise how bad his back was. When he pulled up after the Guineas he was nearly in tears from the pain.'

Fairy Footsteps provided another link with the past, for Piggott rode her in the famous black and red colours of racing's grand old man, Jim Joel, who had been one of the principal patrons of Sir Noel Murless. And as Lester, with a typical combination of judgement and strength, drove Fairy Footsteps home in front in one of the tightest finishes to a Classic for years (six horses were covered by less than two lengths) there was certainly no sign that the years had begun to take even the minutest toll on his skill.

There was an amusing postscript to the success of Fairy Footsteps, as recalled by a colleague, Colin Fleetwood Jones, who was ghosting a column for Piggott in the *Daily Star* at that time. 'Someone in the *Daily Star* office had made a mistake in the caption under the picture of the Guineas finish,' Fleetwood Jones explains. 'The caption read "Fairy Footsteps winning the 1,000 Guineas at *Newbury*" instead of "Newmarket". That appealed to Lester's sense of humour and he couldn't wait to confront me the following day. "'Ere," he said, grinning wickedly. "That filly must be f—g good. She started at Newbury and still won!"'

There were two more Classics for Piggott in 1981, both gained at the expense of the Swinburn family. Piggott had often ridden for the leading Irish trainer Dermot Weld, and Weld booked him to ride his filly Blue Wind in the Oaks instead of his regular jockey, Walter Swinburn senior. There was the usual outcry, and once again it was misguided, because Swinburn had readily agreed to step down in favour of the acknowledged master of Epsom. Blue Wind scooted home to win very easily, but Swinburn did at least get back aboard when she took the Irish Oaks, so he received fairly hefty compensation.

Swinburn's son, Walter, had been signed up that season to ride for Michael Stoute, one of Cecil's fiercest rivals. Having made a dream start by easing home Shergar in the Derby, Swinburn then followed Piggott's path in getting himself banned for careless riding in Royal Ascot's King Edward VII Stakes. Lester, it

A pair of queens: Piggott wins the Oaks on the Irish-trained filly, Blue Wind (left) in 1981, and on Circus Plume (right) in 1984

100

may be recalled, had been banned for six months over his riding of Never Say Die in the same Ascot event. Swinburn's sentence was a relatively mild six-day suspension, but it meant that he was ineligible to ride Shergar in the Irish Derby. Piggott had ridden frequently for Stoute the previous year – there had been rumours that he would become Stoute's new stable jockey when he left Sangster – and he was the obvious replacement on Shergar, particularly as he had partnered the Aga Khan's precocious colt in both his juvenile races.

Shergar sauntered home at the Curragh; but it was the last race he would win. He failed badly in the St Leger and was retired. He was subsequently abducted from the Aga Khan's stud in Ireland. The IRA was suspected but nothing was ever proved and his body was never found.

As well as Fairy Footsteps and Shergar there were many other cracking good horses to ride that year, including most notably Ardross, who carried Lester to his tenth success in the Ascot Gold Cup. The following year Ardross won the Gold Cup again and was beaten by only a head by Akiyida in the Prix de l'Arc de Triomphe. Charles St George, who bought Ardross as a five-year-old before the start of the 1981 season, said that losing the Arc on Ardross was one of Piggott's rare errors of judgement. 'Ardross was thought to be just an out-and-out stayer and Lester didn't really believe he was good enough to beat the best middle-distance horses in the Arc. In hindsight, Lester probably would have ridden him differently.'

The big bonus for Piggott that year was regaining the jockeys' title after a nine-year gap. The upstarts Eddery and Carson were put firmly in their place as Lester weighed in with what proved to be his third highest tally of 179 winners. The following year his haul was even bigger: 188 successes, only three fewer than his highest total set in 1966.

But if 1982 was a memorable year numerically, it was not a vintage one in terms of cash and kudos. There were no Classic successes in England or Ireland and for the first time in twenty years he did not ride in the Derby after his intended mount, Simply Great, was injured a few days before the race. However, Lester did gallop off with the French 1,000 Guineas on River Lady. And to prove that his ability to winkle out winners across the globe had not been impaired, he picked up the Swedish St Leger on Kansas.

Piggott will remember 1983 for two main reasons – his partnership with the fine colt Teenoso, who carried him to his ninth and possibly easiest Derby triumph, and the bitter severance of his connection with Daniel Wildenstein.

Teenoso was trained by Geoffrey Wragg, who had been assistant to his father Harry, the former champion jockey, for some thirty years until Wragg senior retired at the end of the 1982 season. The debonair Geoff and his charming wife, Trish, were long-standing personal friends of Piggott. They socialised with Lester and Susan regularly and Trish kept Lester's scrapbook for him. The Wraggs revere Lester and are quick to dispel some of the myths that surround him. 'The thing with Lester is that he likes to perpetuate those myths. He likes to be the mystery man,' Geoff says. 'But in reality he does not do many of the things he is supposed to do. For example, he is not mean. He may act that way just for devilment, but he is the first to pick up the tab when we go out for a meal. And it's also a fallacy that he never ate. He had a cigar and a cup of coffee for breakfast, but he would often eat a decent-sized meal at night.'

'Lester has a marvellously dry sense of humour,' Trish says. 'And he is so observant and alert. At the races you might think he is not taking any notice of what is going on around him, but he is taking it all in. On the way home he would keep us amused for hours telling us all sorts of fascinating things about the people he had seen and what they had done.'

Wragg considered Teenoso an outstanding prospect for Epsom and naturally wanted Lester to ride the colt, but Lester was committed to ride for Cecil. So Wragg called up Steve Cauthen and the American rode Teenoso to impressive wins in his first two races of the season. But as the Derby drew closer, Sangster exercised his claim on Cauthen for The Noble Player and Piggott, without an obvious Epsom ride from Cecil's yard, was on the loose.

Piggott's principal prospects at that stage were the 2,000 Guineas runner-up Tolomeo, trained by one of Wragg's Newmarket rivals, Luca Cumani, and Vincent O'Brien's two runners, Salmon Leap and Lomond. 'Lester came and rode Teenoso in a gallop on the Racecourse Side [one of Newmarket's trial grounds] on the Saturday morning before the Derby,' Wragg recalls. 'Teenoso worked very well and Lester told me that he would gallop Tolomeo on Sunday, then speak to Vincent and then let me know his decision later on Sunday.

'Despite his reputation, Lester is a man of his word. If he said he would let you know on a certain day he would never let you down. He rang up on Sunday as agreed and told me he would ride Teenoso. From that moment on I was highly confident we would win the Derby. Even so, I could hardly believe how easily Lester was going as the runners reached the top of the hill. I turned to Trish and said "We'll trot up." She said "There's still a long way to go." But we were always going to win.'

Wragg was not alone in spotting that Piggott had only to make his move to take the race whenever he wanted. The Epsom crowd began to roar its approval as Lester eased Teenoso into the lead after rounding Tattenham Corner. With the colt revelling in the heavy ground it was simply a case of who would finish a distant second as Teenoso strode home in splendid isolation. As Lester jumped down from the back of his ninth Derby winner, he turned to Wragg and said dryly: 'It was easy, wasn't it?'

There was an embarrassing sequel for Wragg, as he explains. 'In the morning I had asked Trish if I should take a suit with me to Epsom, because if we won the race I could hardly go out to celebrate in morning dress. She told me that was being a bit too hopeful, so I didn't bother.

'After the Derby we went back to Lester's flat in London and decided to go to the White Elephant club for a celebratory dinner. I said to Lester that I would feel a proper Charlie wearing tails, so he lent me a grey sweater which was about six sizes too small for me.

'There were a host of celebrities including Roger Moore dining at the White Elephant that evening. Imagine my embarrassment when I walked in wearing this sweater that was halfway up my arms. I apologised to the head waiter, but he was very understanding and in the end we had a thoroughly enjoyable night. At one point in the evening Lester said "It all seems a bit flat now." He was already thinking about what he was going to ride the following day.'

Piggott's courage and humour are further illustrated by the events surrounding Teenoso's victory in the Grand Prix de Saint-Cloud the following year. This success and his subsequent triumph over a high-class field in the King George VI and Queen Elizabeth Diamond Stakes underlined Teenoso's outstanding merit, something that has never been fully acknowledged.

'After the horses had paraded before the start of the Saint-Cloud race, they turned round to canter down to the start and one of the French runners backed into our fellow,' Wragg recalls. 'Teenoso threw his head up and hit Lester in the face. He fell off with blood pouring from his eye, but he still had hold of the reins.

'A doctor and an ambulance crew arrived down at the start. They wanted to cart Lester off to hospital and put stitches in his eye. Lester brushed them aside and before anyone could do anything about it he was back on board Teenoso and gone.

'During the race his eye was bleeding so much that he couldn't see out of it after they had gone half a mile and he rode the last mile of the race with one eye. He produced the most magnificent finish to get home by a short neck, and when he pulled his goggles down afterwards blood poured out. It splattered everywhere, all over his colours. He looked as if he'd been in the biggest fight of all time.

'Later on, Lester and I took a taxi to the airport with Eric Moller, Teenoso's owner. Moller had a silver cup and a plate and I said that I thought the cup was supposed to be for me. Moller turned to Lester, and said "Didn't you get a prize, Leslie?" [Leslie was a nickname used by Moller and some of Piggott's colleagues]. Lester, with his eye looking a real mess, replied quick as a flash: "No, but they're going to give me the Croix de Guerre!"'

It was Wragg's father, Harry, who sprang to Piggott's defence after an incident that was instrumental in souring Daniel Wildenstein's relationship with Piggott. Wildenstein, the wealthy Parisian art dealer, was notorious for changing trainers and jockeys the way other people change their underwear. His high-handedness led to racing journalist Alistair Down coming out with a memorable line at the Frenchman's expense. Down suggested that the traditional directive 'Horses away', which is given to stable staff after the horses have been standing in

French dressing-down: Piggott wins on Vacarme at Goodwood in 1983, but he was demoted by the stewards and his riding of the colt also incurred the displeasure of owner Daniel Wildenstein, who severed their association later that year

the unsaddling enclosure after a race, might be replaced with one word – 'Wildenstein'.

The incident that first ruffled Wildenstein's feathers concerned Piggott's riding of his good two-year-old Vacarme at Goodwood in July 1983. Piggott appeared to ride a beautifully judged race to win on Vacarme, who was a white-hot favourite at 3–1 on. However, the stewards decided that Piggott had interfered with Pacific King when he made his move on the inside and disqualified Vacarme from first place, suspending Lester for five days for careless riding. Wildenstein was furious because he felt that Piggott should have made his challenge on the outside instead of taking an unnecessarily risky passage on the inner. Cecil was apparently none too pleased either, but Lester had won the race the way he thought best and that should have been good enough. The race was a rough one overall and the stewards seemed to be less than even-handed in casting Lester as the villain. Wragg senior, once the acknowledged master of the late swoop, certainly felt there had been a travesty of justice.

Geoff Wragg says: 'I had watched the Goodwood event and afterwards I said to myself "Lester didn't half ride a good race. He was bloody brilliant." I couldn't really see that he had interfered with anything. The funny thing was that when I got home from Goodwood I have never known my father so upset about anything in his life. He kept on about it for weeks.

'Dad said, "When you achieve something like that you say to yourself 'Christ, I brought it off'. Then they go and hit you with a hammer. I really felt for Lester. I can't understand how the stewards could be so bloody stupid."'

Wildenstein finally froze Piggott out some two months later, accusing him of reneging on an agreement to ride his filly, All Along, in the Prix de l'Arc de Triomphe. Piggott had agreed to ride Sheikh Mohammed's filly, Awaasif, several weeks before the Arc, but about a week before the race he received a phone call from Patrick Biancone, All Along's trainer, asking him if he would ride Wildenstein's filly. Piggott apparently told Biancone that he was committed to Awaasif if she came through her final gallop satisfactorily. With the slightly farcical combination of Piggott's nasal monotone and Biancone's fractured English, some sort of communications breakdown was almost inevitable and Biancone came off the phone believing that he had secured the maestro's services. When Piggott announced that he was staying with Awaasif, Wildenstein almost blew a gasket. 'Piggott gave us his word that he would ride All Along and he has gone back on it,' Wildenstein said. 'He will never ride for me again. He is a genius but I don't want to have to dance to his music.'

Wildenstein also had the last word in the Arc itself when Walter Swinburn urged All Along to victory, with Piggott an impotent onlooker as he laboured home unplaced on Awaasif. Piggott's decision had cost him a massive pay cheque and he was not a happy man.

Wildenstein's refusal to allow Piggott on his horses created an embarrassing situation for Cecil, who trained more than twenty of them. Cecil was ordered whenever possible to secure either Swinburn or Cauthen to carry the dark and light blue colours during 1984. The arrangement soon proved untenable and before the season had reached the halfway point Cecil had reluctantly informed Piggott that their contract would not be renewed in 1985 and signed Cauthen up as his new stable jockey. The irony was that almost exactly a year later Wildenstein removed all his horses from Cecil's yard.

So Piggott was out on his ear once again; but he could afford to shrug his shoulders at Wildenstein, for the season proved to be no disaster. Cauthen won his first jockeys' title that year, but Piggott still managed 100 winners for third place and, far more important, he wrote himself into the record books with two more Classic triumphs. The first came on Circus Plume, who carried Piggott to a momentous triumph in the Oaks. Trained by John Dunlop, Circus Plume looked likely to cruise home when Lester sent her to the front in the straight, but when the rank outsider Media Luna came at her it seemed she would be caught for sure. Once again, however, Lester's unfathomable x-factor turned apparent defeat into victory.

Circus Plume's victory gave Piggott his twenty-seventh English Classic win,

Darrel McHargue, the American rider, received much sympathy after he had been 'jocked off' Commanche Run by Piggott in the 1984 St Leger. However, McHargue said he would have done the same thing in Piggott's position

equalling the record set by Frank Buckle 157 years previously. Three months later he had surpassed it, taking the St Leger for the eighth time on Commanche Run after using up as much energy to talk himself on to the horse in place of Darrel McHargue (see Chapter Four) as he did to fight off challengers in the Doncaster straight.

The following year, Commanche Run and Piggott teed themselves up for a £1 million bonus. That was the sum offered to any horse that could win the Benson and Hedges Gold Cup at York, the Phoenix Champion Stakes in Ireland and the Dubai Champion Stakes at Newmarket. Lester and Commanche Run picked off the first two events, but the colt was past his best at Newmarket and never really looked like troubling the brilliant filly, Pebbles, and the Derby winner, Slip Anchor.

So the million pounds went begging; but race fans would gladly have coughed up that sum and a lot more besides to overturn the worst piece of news they had heard for years. At the beginning of 1985, it was announced that this was to be Piggott's last season in the saddle. He was to hang up his riding boots and switch to training at the yard he had already prepared for the purpose at his home, Eve Lodge in Hamilton Road, Newmarket.

The news of Lester's departure had been broken by Peter O'Sullevan in his final column for the *Daily Express* on 19 January. O'Sullevan was the only journalist who genuinely had Piggott's confidence and his announcement seemed 100 per cent authentic.

'When I broke the story Lester made a vehement denial and I couldn't understand why,' O'Sullevan says. 'He had told me quite definitely that it was his last season and had even said to me "We must share a horse when I start training." It transpired that the reason for his apparent backtracking was that he had signed a contract with the *Express*'s sister paper, the *Daily Star*, who expected all Piggott exclusives themselves, and there was a hell of a row. The *Star* printed a strenuous denial, and three months later they ran their own "exclusive" announcing Lester's retirement.'

Even for those who accepted that O'Sullevan's story was genuine, it was impossible not to doubt whether Piggott would really go through with it. So many times in the past there had been rumours that he was to give up, particularly during times of trouble, and he himself had said on many occasions that he would not go on beyond such and such an age – only to sail on serenely when his time was supposedly up.

As the 1985 campaign unfolded, however, there was no sign that Lester was going to pull back from the brink this time. Attention was focused on his every move to an even greater degree than usual. There was a much publicised match race with the former champion jumps jockey, John Francome, who had just retired after a career that had carried him into the record books and the gossip columns.

The event dubbed the Walton Hall Duel of Champions filled lowly Warwick racecourse to bursting point on a memorable evening in May. Lester on The Liquidator held off John on Shangoseer in a tense battle that was certainly not a put-up job. It was good clean fun, but tinged with sadness as another indication that Piggott's professional days were numbered. His adoring public could not believe it was happening, but just in case it really was Lester's last stand they treated each and every glimpse of him as a moment to treasure.

There were only thirty-four wins from 257 rides in that final season, but among them were particular gems to savour, such as a last Classic flourish on Shadeed in the 2,000 Guineas, another 'gift' from young Walter Swinburn. Piggott had been due to ride Bairn, owned by Sheikh Mohammed, with Swinburn on Shadeed, who carried the colours of the Sheikh's older brother, Maktoum Al Maktoum. When Swinburn was banned for three weeks by the Epsom stewards, ruling him out of the Newmarket Classic, there were rapid consultations among the Arabs and their advisers and it was decided to switch Piggott to Shadeed, who was a hot favourite and engage Willie Carson for Bairn.

The race looked like being another breeze for Lester when he cruised into the lead two furlongs from home. However, Carson came after Piggott with a sense of purpose that suggested he was determined finally to banish the memory of that afternoon eight years previously when Lester and The Minstrel achieved the impossible in cutting down Hot Grove in the Derby.

Poor Willie came out second best again. Piggott kept Shadeed going to win by a head and Michael Stoute, Shadeed's trainer, said a silent prayer of thanks that Lester had switched to his horse. Shadeed had become extremely worked up in the pre-race parade and Stoute had dispatched him down to the start before the rest of the field. It was a move that cost him £550 and led to revision of the rule governing parades.

'I was awfully glad Lester was on our side that day,' Stoute says. 'Shadeed was not spot on for the Guineas and he was definitely not the horse he was when he won the Craven Stakes. Once again Lester made the difference between victory and defeat. Over the years he has done that so many times.'

Shadeed did not in fact complete Piggott's international Classic haul. The same year he took the French Oaks on Lypharita and provided the Australians with a demonstration of his magic when he purloined their Oaks on Centaurea. And there were three more successes to add to his tally at Royal Ascot, where he was top or joint top jockey eighteen times.

But the end was indeed nigh. It arrived at Nottingham on 29 October and with all the publicity it generated, it could not have been upstaged by anything much less than a world war. Among the eulogies in the press one of the most memorable came from the eloquent pen of Simon Barnes, who wrote in *The Times*: 'Piggott is not just the greatest horseman we shall ever see. He is probably the most complete sportsman we will ever see as well . . . He has dedicated his life to eradicating the chance element from the most chancy business in the world.'

Barnes went on: '"Well Lester?", someone said at the press conference held before racing began, "is there anything you haven't done as a jockey that you hope to do when you become a trainer?" Lester replied "Eat". Piggott has lived at starvation levels for over thirty years. By doing so he has managed to dominate his sport for three decades. What sportsman will ever be able to match such a claim?'

Among the stream of telegrams that were dispatched to Lester there was one from the Queen Mother telling him 'You will be sorely missed.' To Piggott's admirers, not just at Nottingham but all across the country, that must have seemed like the understatement of the decade.

Piggott rode five horses at Nottingham and managed one last win for the dewy-eyed gallery, leading all the way on Full Choke to bring his total of British wins to 4,349. The watching world held its collective breath as Lester went out to get the leg up on his last ride of all, a horse called Wind From The West. It seemed too much like fiction to hope that he would exit on a winner, but there was a hint that he might have some supernatural assistance. Wind From The West was trained by Patrick Haslam at Pegasus stables in Newmarket, built in 1886 by Fred Archer, the greatest jockey of the nineteenth century. Archer, said to be a hero of Piggott, shot himself in a fit of depression two years later and his ghost is said to walk the stables.

Sadly, Piggott never had a ghost of a chance on Wind From The West as 22-year-old Tony McGlone drove Gurteen Boy well clear. 'Piggott is a true professional and so am I. He wouldn't do me a favour and I wouldn't do him one,' McGlone said. That seemed a rather prosaic explanation of one of the most poignant moments in the history of sport.

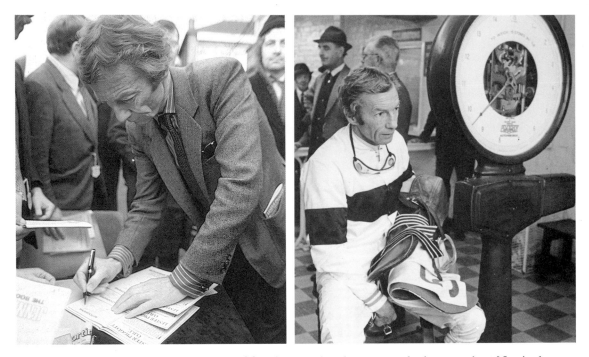

Signing off: Lester kept a vast queue of fans happy when he autographed racecards at Nottingham on the day of his retirement and he weighs in after his 'last' winner, Full Choke

In terms of emotional content Piggott's last ride could be compared to George Best's last shot at goal, Rocky Marciano's final right hook or Len Hutton's last cover drive. Yet there was more to it even than that. For those three spellbinding decades alluded to by Barnes, Piggott *was* English racing. He would still be a part of the scene, it was true, but his new role could never compensate remotely for the old. Even if he trained a thousand winners, it could not possibly equal one blood-stirring ride in the Derby.

Yes, it really was over, but many of us simply could not believe what we were seeing. Earlier, Lester had sat down to sign autographs for a queue of fans that seemed to wind into the distance like the Great Wall of China. At the end of the day a steel band played 'For He's a Jolly Good Fellow' and with a last dash from the weighing room he was into a helicopter and away.

As Lester became just a speck on the horizon a feeling of enormous loss descended. Whatever they said about the man and whatever he might have done to incur the wrath of those who set themselves up as moral arbiters, he was still regarded with infinitely more affection than any ordinary straight-down-the-middle player. Lester had brought excitement into the lives of millions; nothing and no one could possibly take his place. At that moment, the title of David Niven's autobiography, *Bring on the Empty Horses*, came to mind; from that day on, the horses would seem very empty indeed without Lester.

CHAPTER SEVEN
THE TAXMAN'S AXE

If that last glimpse of Lester Piggott disappearing into the evening sky high above Nottingham racecourse was a poignant moment for his admirers, it was nothing compared to the traumatic sight almost exactly two years later of his gaunt features staring out through the window of a prison bus as he was whisked away from Ipswich Crown Court to begin a three-year gaol term for income tax and VAT offences.

When Piggott retired from the saddle he had amassed a personal fortune estimated at around £20 million. Much has been made of the fact that he hoarded his cash and so he did, but that is not a particularly unusual trait: if we are honest, most of us would admit to being averse to parting with our hard-earned cash, and Lester had more excuse than most for wanting to keep a tight rein on his money. His parents had drummed into him from a very early age that caution should be his byword because there were many unscrupulous people in racing just waiting to relieve him of what he earned. Lester was to discover the painful truth of that advice on many occasions.

Robert Armstrong, Piggott's brother-in-law, offers an intriguingly different psychological perspective on Lester's frugality. 'Because Lester had to starve himself all his life, the business of being ultra-careful with his money was his subconscious way of feeling he would never have to go short in the future,' Armstrong says. That might seem like confused logic at first, but the more you think about it the more it makes sense.

The line between frugality and meanness is one that Lester is frequently said to have crossed, but on the basis of the evidence that is unfair, even if there was at least one precedent that might have suggested an inherited tendency in that direction. The incident concerned Lester's grandfather, Ernie, after he had ridden one of his three Grand National winners. The winning National jockey traditionally would send a case of champagne to the weighing room for the other riders, but on this occasion there was no sign of Ernie or the champagne. A search party was sent out and Ernie was located hiding away in a cafe sipping a cup of tea!

Bill Rickaby, Lester's cousin, was once quoted as saying: 'He relishes each crisp fiver like some jewel, for money is his staff of life and he ekes it out as sparingly as a man faced with fifty years of unpensionable retirement.' Strong stuff indeed, but undoubtedly an exaggeration.

There is a myriad of Lester stories involving his obsession with money and his crafty avoidance of paying for things like meals and taxis, but most of those are clearly apocryphal. As we have heard from Susan, Lester is as generous as the next man when it comes to handing out presents and buying things for his family. And as Geoff Wragg and others have pointed out, for every instance of Lester allegedly not paying his share there is at least one example of him being the first to pick up the tab. On the occasions when Lester has appeared to duck out of his responsibilities in that area it has mostly been out of sheer devilment combined with an eagerness to play up to his own image.

Piggott's supposed financial wizardry in areas outside racing was even more of an illusion. Lester made his fortune out of racing and nothing else, even though he was supposed to have read the *Financial Times* more diligently than the *Sporting Life* and known more about share prices than pedigrees. Harry Carr, the former royal jockey, said in an interview in the *Observer*: 'When you are in an hotel with Lester you will find him in the morning with the *Financial Times* up in front of his face, and a pot of black coffee beside the bed and one of those big cigars in his mouth. He can tell you the exchange rate in any part of the world.' The truth was very different. Charles St George, the wealthy businessman who knew Lester as a close friend and patron virtually since the beginning of his career, said that Piggott's reputation as a financial sage was totally misleading. St George said that Piggott merely dabbled on the stock market with a 'success' rate that would definitely not have enabled him to give up his day job. 'All this stuff about the *Financial Times* is nonsense,' he said. 'Lester was not a financial wizard. He used to fool about with shares.'

Furthermore, Piggott was involved in several disastrous financial ventures, notably those involving Lloyd's syndicates, some of which were run by St George's Oakeley Vaughan Agency, and which cost famous-name participants millions of pounds in losses. Along with Steve Cauthen, Piggott also lost a substantial sum of money in a grandiose but ill-conceived oil deal dreamed up by a dubious character named Sam Bernard who charmed his way into Piggott's confidence.

Michael Watt, who was Piggott's business manager for ten years, also dismisses the notion that he was knowledgeable and astute on financial matters. 'When I first met Piggott he had a stack of commercial propositions from other people which I was supposed to advise him on,' he says. 'However, he suppressed a lot of information and did not tell me everything I needed to know. He frequently acted on his instincts rather than listening to my advice and would then come to me to sort out the mess.

'Piggott was attracted to people who offered to bring him vast financial rewards and he would go for deals that were unreal. They were the sort of deals that a normally sensitive, intelligent businessman would have suspected as being too good to be true, offering massive returns with no apparent risk. The problem was that Piggott was so totally engrossed in horse racing and breeding that he lost sight of what went on around him outside that closed world of his. He couldn't understand other people being interested in anything that didn't somehow involve racing. He inadvertently taught me that I should be grateful for a lot of things that he wasn't – the simple, everyday things of life which he didn't have time to appreciate. He became a victim of his own tunnel vision because he didn't have enough experience outside racing to suss out those people offering the phony deals. He was totally single-minded and in that sense he was the complete professional. If you could design the perfect sportsman, motivated by success and the money it brings, it would be Lester Piggott.'

Watt, a New Zealander who came up the hard way, is still saddled with the tag of Piggott's ex-business manager, but he also handled the affairs of other leading sports personalities such as Severiano Ballesteros and Nigel Mansell and now runs one of the world's two largest sports television companies. 'I chose to go my separate way from Piggott a year before the revenue trial when I was becoming more and more involved with my television business,' Watt explains. 'Not long before his arrest I had told him that I was worried about the direction in which he was going and he said, "You worry too much". I knew there was trouble coming, you could sniff it in the air. When they raided my offices I had already made sure that everything was in perfect order.

'Piggott thought he was above it all and that he could carry on in that manner and nothing would happen. He assumed there was one system for the privileged few and another for the masses. There was a twilight world around English racing at that time and the one good thing that happened as a result of Piggott's conviction was that the racing industry was forced to clean itself up.'

Sources close to Watt have said that if Piggott had allowed him to take complete responsibility for all his financial affairs he would never have landed himself in hot water over his tax. 'I don't regret any of the trials and tribulations. I look back on the times I spent with Piggott with lots of affection and I particularly remember his tremendous sense of humour,' Watt says. 'The problems arose because I was a total friend, but not a total commercial minder.'

It was one of those dubious individuals alluded to by Watt, who appear fleetingly on the racing scene like brightly coloured butterflies, who was to bring about Piggott's conviction for tax fraud. Lester's nemesis was instigated by one Melvyn Walters, a convicted criminal, bloodstock agent and would-be high-roller. Piggott was caught in the crossfire when Walters sought revenge on racing's establishment for a failed bloodstock deal. The irony was that Walters never intended Piggott to be his target.

Piggott was the prize catch netted by Operation Centaur, a joint Inland

Revenue and Customs and Excise inquiry in which sixteen leading trainers and jockeys were interviewed after a letter from Henry Cecil was leaked to the newspapers at the instigation of Walters. In common with other patrons of Cecil's Warren Place establishment – he had a filly called Bright Crocus in training with Cecil in his wife's name – Walters received a letter from the trainer before the start of the 1982 Flat season setting out 'private' arrangements to pay Piggott a retainer over and above the normal jockeys' fees and percentages.

Under Jockey Club rules a jockey could enter into any such arrangements provided they were registered with Weatherbys, the Club's secretariat. As mentioned in an earlier chapter, the practice of giving extras to riders in the form of so-called 'presents', usually cash or shares in stallions, was a long-established one. By tradition these presents were regarded as a perk that did not need to be officially declared. It was understood that the services of a leading jockey like Piggott had to be bought in this way and, as we have seen, shares in stallions alone could be worth a fortune to the men who rode them.

Cecil's list of patrons read like an extract from *Who's Who* or *Debrett*, but many of these establishment figures, who included members of the Jockey Club, were surprisingly naïve and unsophisticated and in spite of a lifelong involvement with racing needed to have such arrangements spelled out to them. Cecil's solicitor therefore drafted a letter asking for payments in cash and shares in big-race winners when they were syndicated as stallions in addition to the usual retainer and fees. The letter, which was not seen by Piggott before it went out, was accompanied by a note advising the recipients to destroy the letter once they had read it.

By chance Walters had kept his copy of the note and letter and he subsequently used it as his trump card in a bitter dispute between Alchemy (International) Ltd, a company of which he was a director, and Tattersalls, the leading bloodstock sales company. It was as a result of this dispute that Cecil and Piggott were drawn into a sequence of events that became far bigger than anyone, including Walters, could possibly have imagined.

It all began when Alchemy, a Kentucky-based bloodstock company, submitted a colt by Riverman for sale at the Tattersalls Highflyer Sale, the country's most prestigious sale of yearlings, in September 1983. The colt had been bought as a foal in the United States the previous year for $95,000 and he was then sent to the Cliff Stud in Yorkshire, which is run by Henry Cecil's twin brother, David, and jointly owned by the two of them. David Cecil supervised the nurturing of the Riverman colt for the Highflyer Sale the following year. The idea was to sell him for a vast profit, a practice known as 'pin-hooking' which has proved extremely lucrative for certain shrewd judges of immature horseflesh.

The atmosphere at any renowned international bloodstock sale is always heady, to say the least. Watching the rich, filthy rich and oil rich gathering to do battle with cheque books that could probably pay off a good proportion of the national debt between them makes compulsive viewing. Many of the gliterati are merely there to be seen and the scent of money hangs in the air like expensive perfume. And by any standards the 1983 Highflyer Sale was a momentous one. Tattersalls' record price for a yearling, 640,000 guineas, had been broken twice with the sale of colts by the Derby winner, Troy, and the American sire, General Assembly, for 1,020,000 guineas and 1,400,000 guineas respectively. The excitement had still not died down when Alchemy's Riverman colt entered the ring to come under the critical gaze of the gallery.

When the colt was knocked down for 430,000 guineas Walters and his Alchemy partners were looking at a fairly healthy profit on their original $95,000 purchase. Then came the bad news that Tattersalls could not trace the man who had made the final bid. He had disappeared without signing the sales slip and could not be found anywhere. The auctioneers pondered this extraordinary situation and decided that in view of the fact that it was late in the day and many leading bidders would have gone home, their first course of action was to offer the colt to the underbidder and make up the difference of 10,000 guineas to Alchemy themselves. Omar Assi, the underbidder, would not play ball, however, as there was a feeling that he had been 'run up' in order to get a higher price, something that had happened to wealthy purchasers many times in the past. Tattersalls therefore re-submitted the colt for sale two days later; this time he fetched only 200,000 guineas. Walters was furious and Alchemy decided to sue Tattersalls for the shortfall of 230,000 guineas. The case came to the High Court almost two and a half years later.

Jimmy Flood, an Irish gambler, had eventually been tagged as the man who made the final bid for the Riverman colt. Alchemy sued Tattersalls for the 230,000 guineas, alleging negligence in conducting its business, and also put in a claim against Flood. After a hearing lasting thirteen days, Tattersalls was cleared of negligence and Alchemy was ordered to pay the costs of the case, estimated at almost £250,000. Walters' company was awarded 230,000 guineas damages against Flood, which was of little consequence as he was unable to pay.

Long before the case came to court, Walters had asked Cecil to intervene on his behalf. Cecil refused and Walters became so incensed by the trainer's attitude that in 1984 he arranged for the letter concerning the cash payments to Piggott to be circulated to various Fleet Street newspapers through two of his business associates, Michael Mendoza and Samuel Hyams. The *Daily Mirror* and the *Daily Express* did not publish the story, but it appeared in the *People* in February 1985, some four months before the *Alchemy* v. *Tattersalls* case reached the High Court. In between these two events and as a result of the *People* article, Cecil had been fined £2,000 by the Jockey Club for breaching rule 75 governing retainers for jockeys.

The tax authorities had been aware of the cash payments system in racing for some time before the Cecil letter and the publication of that document in the

People gave them just the impetus they needed to mount a massive inquiry. The *People* handed over its dossier on the matter to the Inland Revenue and Operation Centaur was set in train. Scores of officers were involved, notably the crack investigative men who belonged to the 'C' team of the Customs and Excise, who have far greater powers than the Revenue. The operation shook British racing to its foundations. Just about everybody who was anybody in racing was interviewed, including members of the Jockey Club.

In a synchronised swoop that came to be known in racing as 'The Invasion' officers descended on the homes of leading owners, trainers and jockeys, including the likes of the Maktoum brothers and Robert Sangster, who all readily agreed to make available full details of any payments to jockeys. As well as Cecil and Piggott, the professionals who were quizzed included the top jockeys Pat Eddery, Willie Carson and Steve Cauthen and leading trainers John Dunlop, Guy Harwood and Dick Hern, who then had charge of the Queen's horses.

But Piggott was the man that the powers behind Operation Centaur really wanted. During his final season in the saddle in 1985 they followed up the revelations in the *People* and set to work trying to prove that Piggott had received millions in regular but undeclared extra payments which he had been salting away somewhere. This involved months of wading through form books to examine every ride Piggott had had since 1970, and totalling up the prize money and the fees as recorded at Weatherbys. They were then able to compare his officially recorded income and his VAT returns with what he actually received, most notably the massive sums associated with shares in stallions he had ridden.

Piggott had already been the subject of two previous investigations by the Revenue. The first, between 1970 and 1973, found that Piggott had understated his income by £83,000. Piggott swore then that he had disclosed everything. 'Sadly, that was far from the truth,' the court was told at Piggott's trial in 1987. The second investigation, between 1981 and 1983, revealed two offshore companies in the Bahamas, Lambay and Zeus, which concealed Piggott's earnings from UK and overseas rides. Once again Piggott paid up what he owed, declaring that he had only one bank account, with the Natwest in Newmarket, which contained £28,000. When after the second investigation he was ordered to put the Bahamian companies back onshore, he opened another offshore company in Panama called Western Agency Incorporated to carry on perpetrating the fraud.

Having collated sufficient evidence against Piggott, the Customs men had paid a visit to his house in Newmarket in January 1986 and seized accounts and documents relating to Piggott and his company, L. K. Piggott Ltd. The officers quizzed Piggott for two days during which time he made what were described as 'limited admissions'. They were amazed that Piggott had almost total recall of all the thousands of races he had ridden in but virtually no memory of the details surrounding his financial affairs.

It was during this visit that officers discovered three guns, one of them an antique revolver, and almost 500 rounds of ammunition in a locked cabinet. Piggott was subsequently fined £1,000 by Newmarket magistrates on charges arising out of his non-possession of a proper firearms licence.

Following the raid Piggott continued to lie about his affairs. Price Waterhouse, a leading firm of accountants, was called in to investigate and settle his account with the Revenue but still Piggott managed to conceal more than £2 million from them in seventeen secret bank accounts with the Allied Irish Bank, some of them in false names. When this deception was discovered, apparently as an indirect result of investigations by Special Branch into terrorist activities, any hope of a compromise deal was scuppered and the prosecution that stunned racing was instigated.

On 19 December 1986, the racing world reverberated with the news that Piggott had been arrested on a charge of making a false statement with intent to defraud the Inland Revenue. When he appeared at Newmarket Magistrates' Court bail was set at £1 million, the highest ever demanded by magistrates. There followed a hectic scramble to raise the money in time and eventually he was released after signing over the deeds to his house and stables, with Cecil and St George each putting up surety of £125,000. Bail was reduced to £500,000 three days later by the High Court in London and Piggott was allowed to report to the police monthly instead of weekly. On 19 March 1987, Piggott appeared before the Magistrates' Court again; he was remanded until 7 May and his bail further reduced to £250,000.

It soon became obvious that Piggott was in deep, deep trouble. His knack of landing on his feet might have worked on the track, but it seemed nothing could save him from the full force of a legal system that was about to throw the book at him. He faced eleven further charges in a joint prosecution by the Inland Revenue and Customs and Excise. These concerned undeclared income of £3,750,000, of which the Revenue was claiming £2 million in unpaid tax and £800,000 in interest.

There was also an outstanding amount of £140,000 in VAT, which might have seemed relatively insignificant, but it underlined the fact that while the Revenue will allow an almost indefinite amount of rope in certain cases, the Customs and Excise adopt a far harder line. Piggott's much quoted remark 'Everyone owes tax, don't they?' contains a large measure of the truth in terms of income tax, but you certainly cannot say the same about VAT. The much-maligned men of the Revenue are pussycats compared to the hard men of the VAT squad, so once they became involved Piggott's number was up.

As if he did not have enough on his plate already, Piggott was also hit by rumours concerning betting and bookmakers in the months leading up to the trial. The *People* was supposed to have had in its possession a tape recording which indicated that Piggott had been involved in betting contrary to the Rules of

Racing. The Jockey Club's Security Department launched an inquiry, but no action was taken.

There was also a rumour linking Piggott with Ladbrokes, which saw over £100 millon wiped off the share value of the big bookmaking and hotel chain in one day. The late Ryan Price once said that the public like to see skulduggery everywhere in racing and Piggott had always been a major target for the snipers. It takes more than a few well-aimed words to knock Piggott out of his stride and he simply accepted the innuendo and malice as a price to be paid for being a superstar in a jealous and money-dominated world.

Piggott was originally committed for trial at the Old Bailey, but six weeks later the trial was switched to Ipswich Crown Court. The date was set for Friday 23 October. Nothing could now halt Lester's downhill ride to disaster, yet no one in racing could really bring themselves to believe the seriousness of his plight.

Lester's demeanour remained as impassive and unfathomable as ever throughout the period leading up to the trial and he carried on the business of supervising his training operation with conspicuous success (see next chapter). There was certainly no indication that he was bothered about the outcome, even though he had apparently been made aware that he was odds-on to be sent to gaol. St George recalled how Piggott's humour never left him all through that time of

The weight of evidence is heavily against Piggott as the lawyers arrive at Ipswich Crown Court for his trial with cases full of documents

appalling pressure, citing an occasion not long before the trial when Lester came up to Cecil's house for breakfast before setting off for London to discuss various matters with his accountants and solicitors. 'Lester paused in the doorway on his way out and turned to Henry. "Do me a favour, Henry," he said. "While I'm away don't write any more letters."'

When the unthinkable happened it took even those outside racing by surprise, particularly with regard to the severity of the sentence. The day after the trial, under the banner headline 'Lester's Torment', the *Racing Post*'s lead story started: 'Lester Piggott begins a three-year jail sentence today, his career in ruins, his reputation in tatters. Piggott, the biggest name in racing, finally paid the price for years of income tax and VAT evasion.' Other sub-headlines in the paper talked of 'Racing's Sadness' and 'Lester's Darkest Day'.

The outcome of the trial was never really in doubt from the moment Anthony Hidden QC rose to his feet to put the case for the prosecution. Even as the charges were read out – they had been reduced from twelve to ten – it was clear that there could be no defence, only an attempt at mitigation. Piggott, who had been allowed to sit in the witness box instead of the dock, leaned forward with his chin resting in his hands, listening intently but without any definable expression. We could only guess at his thoughts, but Lester being Lester we would probably have been wrong in our assumptions.

Speaking in carefully measured tones that seemed to accentuate the weight of his case, Hidden began to reveal to the packed courtroom how Piggott had defrauded the Inland Revenue and Customs and Excise of vast amounts of money during his long career, and reminded the court that Piggott had escaped prosecution during two previous Inland Revenue inquiries. Hidden said that Piggott had failed to declare income of £3,118,788, on which he had evaded income tax of £1,730,290. This consisted of £2,237,234 income for L. K. Piggott Ltd, on which £1,151,258 tax was unpaid, and personal income of £881,554, on which £579,032 was owed. VAT amounting to £140,836 had also been evaded. Hidden then told the court of Piggott's declaration that he held only one bank account when he in fact held seventeen others; and that he had also failed to declare business interests in the Cayman Islands, the Isle of Man, Jersey and Dublin.

Piggott had also told the Revenue, Hidden continued, that he had been receiving only £10,000 per season from Henry Cecil as a retainer, whereas he in fact had a private arrangement to receive £45,000 extra as well as additional sums for races which he won or was placed in and also shares in stallions he rode. Piggott had also kept quiet about money given to him by third parties from successful bets on horses he was riding.

Hidden went on to say that Piggott's previous settlement with the Inland Revenue in April 1983 (the second of the two earlier investigations) was made on the basis that he had made a complete disclosure of his tax affairs. 'Sadly, he had not. Subsequent disclosures in 1986 have revealed the settlement was made on a false basis and that Mr Piggott failed to reveal the true extent of his income and assets,' Hidden said, and continued, 'It has regrettably to be said that there is a theme running through the defendant's dealings with the Inland Revenue. And that is his persistent failure, even when claiming to do so, to make full disclosure of his assets and income to the Inland Revenue. On a number of occasions subsequent revelations have shown that the claims to be making full disclosure were very far from the truth.'

When Hidden sat down after well over an hour of mostly solid narrative, punctuated by the kind of abstruse dialogue with the judge that outsiders tend to find amusing, the atmosphere was one of stunned disbelief. The dossier of evidence against Piggott came as no surprise, but listening to Hidden putting it before the court in such minute detail and with such unyielding purpose was like watching a noose being tightened around Piggott's neck. Metaphorically speaking, Lester was already as good as hanged. The only question was whether John Matthew QC, Piggott's counsel, could extract some degree of leniency from the bewigged adjudicator on the bench.

In making his plea of mitigation, Matthew must have felt rather like a man in a suit of armour trying to swim the Channel. 'My lord, every so often courts are faced with what can only be described as an overwhelming personal tragedy for which, on the face of it, there does not appear to be any reasonable explanation. And this is one of those occasions,' Matthew began.

'As a jockey he had really dominated his profession for thirty years . . . an incomparable genius on the back of the horse, but while he can thrill the crowds in that way, he was by no means a charismatic person himself. I think some have alleged him to be shrewd and clever, based no doubt upon his superb judgement and dedication as a rider. The fact is . . . that generally speaking, in life away from horses, I stress those words "in life away from horses", he is a man of limited intellectual capacity, in the low/average range of intelligence, which . . . will have been lowered more in the recent years by a degree of brain damage resulting from head injuries which had been caused over the period by a number of substantial falls [Matthew was quoting from a report by a Professor Russell, which he gave to the judge].

'No doubt . . . because of his deafness and resulting speech disability he has never been an easy person with whom to communicate. Therefore he has few real friends,' Matthew went on. 'Even those few feel they don't really know him and speak at times of finding it impossible to understand his thinking, reactions and behaviour. Basically he is accepted as being a loner and a very secret man by nature.

'It was not only his difficulty in hearing which turned him inwards upon himself, but his upbringing; the fact that he was an only child, the very nature of his jockey's life, so much so that even his wife, who hears what I say, has herself sometimes wondered whether she really knows him and understands on occasions really what makes him tick.'

Matthew then turned his attention to Piggott's hoarding of money and attempted to relate it to his lifetime of battling to keep his body some two stone below his natural body weight. 'He systematically starved himself. One of his friends and contemporaries described it as him waging a war on his body . . . Hoarding is a well-known symptom in those who deprive themselves of food. An anorexic tends to behave in that sort of way or even to steal.' Matthew said.

An article by Anne Spackman in the *Independent* the day after Piggott's trial discussed a report in 1950 by Ancel Keys of the University of Minnesota, which showed that men who volunteered to deprive themselves of food developed a sudden obsessive interest in collecting all sorts of objects, ranging from kitchen utensils to second-hand clothes. The report was cited by Dr Peter Cooper of Cambridge University, who lectures in psychopathology and is an expert in eating disorders. Dr Cooper had been interviewing jockeys as part of a study of the psychological effects of dieting.

Matthew then proceeded to go through the charges and referred to 'the Henry Cecil arrangement . . . the letter which was circulated to the owners My lord, perhaps it is this document which gives an insight into the thinking or lack of it, possibly, and the total failure not only by Lester Piggott but many others to appreciate the seriousness and dangers and indeed dishonesty involved in entering into an agreement such as this, because it was done in such a blatantly open way,' Matthew said.

'My lord, racing has always tended to be a cash business and payments of cash which went straight into the pocket had unfortuantely, and I say this quite frankly, become an accepted way of life. So much so that, unbelievably, there was nothing secret or underhand about it, as demonstrated by the way that letter to the owners was produced and distributed.

'The original arrangement as between the jockey and the trainer, drafted by the trainer's solicitor, entered into by the trainer, the terms circulated as I have already indicated openly to owners of standing in the racing world, including members and at least one steward of the Jockey Club, most of whom – I say 'most' because it was not compulsory – made cash payments in this way.

'My lord, the sins of others are certainly vested on this man's shoulders. Did anyone, anyone, advise him against it, professional advisers, lay advisers, trainers, friends, owners, members, stewards? No. Did anyone take any sort of step to prevent it? No.'

Matthew ended his statement by saying: 'At the end of the day, perhaps the predetermined feeling, as Mr Hidden said, which prevails is one of sadness that such an admired and public figure who has given so much pleasure to so many people should now be suffering this public disgrace. He is certainly sad not only because of the suffering, the sorrow and the contrition which he genuinely feels, not only because of the unhappy attention he has caused to be focused on his beloved world of racing, but also because he knows, and he has told me this with conviction, that for him there is no life after racing.

'He has no other life and therefore he is now literally standing with his whole life in the balance. My lord, is he not entitled to say through me: I have served my country as an ambassador abroad and I have served the public with dedication all through my racing life which is now over, and to ask your lordship, have I not built up sufficient credit to stand me in good stead at this moment?

'My lord, I invite your lordship to say that this is a case which in many ways is an exceptional case and therefore it is possible to deal with in what to some might seem to be an exceptionally lenient way. My lord, that is all I say unless I can help your lordship further.'

On taking his seat at the beginning of the trial, Mr Justice Farquharson had tossed a pair of white silk gloves on to his desk; but despite Matthew's eloquent plea the judge gave Piggott anything but the kid glove treatment. He began his summing up by saying: 'Lester Keith Piggott, I suppose that the arguments in your favour could scarcely have been put more attractively than they have during the course of the afternoon and, indeed, during the course of the day because the prosecution have spoken so well of you in your career, having regard to your fame. I take that very much into account.

'Perhaps more than anything, I take into account the substantial repayments you have made to the Inland Revenue including the amounts covered in this indictment. I, of course, pay attention to the fact that you have admitted these offences which I emphasise are offences of dishonesty. It is right perhaps also for me to recognise that a lot of the dishonesty in which you have engaged in your failure to own up to the Inland Revenue as to your various assets, has taken place in a climate where cash payments are not infrequent and often not accounted for.

'On the other hand your fame has resulted in you having a quite enormous income. Tax gathering must depend, must it not, on the honesty of all of us when the demands come in. Up and down the country those who have only a tiny proportion of what you enjoy pay up, loyally meet their obligations. So how can I pass over your case when you had the resources to meet the heavy demands that no doubt would have been made upon you and still have a large amount of money to look after yourself and your family? . . .

'If I were to pass over this it would be an invitation, I feel, for other people to be tempted to dishonour their obligations and try and cheat the Revenue.'

Then the hammer blow fell. Piggott was sentenced to terms of imprisonment amounting to three years on three of the counts and two years for the remaining counts, all the sentences to run concurrently. It represented the most severe sentence ever meted out for tax evasion in Great Britain. Piggott also had to pay the costs of the prosecution, amounting to £34,000, as well as various relatively small fines.

When the judge passed sentence there was still no sign of emotion on Piggott's face. Susan, on the other hand, burst into tears as her husband was led away by a prison officer. She was comforted by a female usher before Piggott's solicitor, Jeremy Richardson, came over to help her from the court.

The next we saw of Lester was when he emerged from the back of the court handcuffed to another prisoner and climbed up on to the bus which took him to Norwich prison. He looked gaunt and pallid, but as reporters and photographers pursued him like a pack of frenzied hounds, he managed a half smile through the bars of the bus window at one photographer who had hijacked a child's bicycle and was pedalling along furiously behind the bus to try to get one final picture scoop.

The racing world, shaken to its roots not just by Lester's sentence but by the ramifications which the case held for their whole way of doing business, began to pour forth sympathetic eulogies, most of them expressing amazement at the severity of Piggott's punishment. Maurice Zilber, the Paris-based, Egyptian-born trainer of Piggott's eighth Derby winner, Empery, gave perhaps the most outraged reaction. 'How can they treat such a great English monument like that? It's terrible, really terrible. One month would have been too much. It's a tragedy for racing.' Henry Cecil typified the general feeling when he said: 'I am very sad and I think it is a very steep sentence. I thought maybe he would get a suspended sentence and get a penalty. In my mind prison will not do him any good at all – he has suffered enough.' And Harry Thomson Jones, another Newmarket trainer, must have echoed the feelings of many when he stated: 'At least Lester worked for his money and risked his neck – not like those who sit behind their desks in the city and just sign slips of paper.' Gerry Bermingham, the MP, said: 'Lester would be better teaching handicapped children about horses than languishing in an overfilled prison.'

The reactions of racing folk were almost all sympathetic, but, to paraphrase Mandy Rice-Davies, they would be, wouldn't they? Generally speaking, the public at large took a far different view of Piggott's crime. To many of them Piggott was just 'that jockey who fiddled his tax'. In a straw poll taken by the *Cambridge Evening News* after the trial, most of those questioned felt he deserved to go to prison, if only because it showed that there was not one law for the poor and another for the rich, although some thought the sentence a bit stiff.

The *Sun*, in its usual way, went completely over the top in its leading article, which stated: 'Lester Piggott, one of the great sportsmen of the century, is behind bars today. In the end the man who was the housewives' favourite turned out to be nothing but a common crook.

'Piggott was a very talented and courageous rider. And he was richly rewarded for his triumphs. But fame and fortune wasn't enough for this greedy man. He wanted even MORE and to get it he was up to every sordid and mean trick in the book. How much of his ill-gotten gains he salted away we shall probably never know. What we do know is that he betrayed the trust of the millions who idolised him.

'The three years' sentence is tough but just. There are many rotten apples in racing. *Piggott was one of them.*'

There are many ways of looking at Piggott's crime. That he deserved to be punished for what he did there can be no doubt. If he was badly advised about his money that cannot be offered as an excuse because he was well aware that what he was doing was illegal. Yet the assertion by Piggott's counsel, John Matthew, that the sins of others were 'vested on Piggott's shoulders', does carry moral weight. Certainly Piggott was made a scapegoat; it is known that as a result of Operation Centaur several leading riders were allowed to pay off their dues without any form of retribution.

In taking under-the-counter payments, Piggott was doing what many others did, only on a larger scale. As Matthew pointed out, cash transactions that were not declared as earnings were the norm in racing. When quizzed about extra cash payments and shares in stallions during the raid on his home, Piggott replied: 'That's what it's all about, isn't it?' And in the context of his particular working environment he was right.

Throughout the world of commerce and industry, millions are making extra cash by illegal means, whether it be through fiddling their expenses, taking backhanders or pilfering office supplies and equipment. The printing industry provided a classic example of this before Rupert Murdoch broke the power of the print unions when he moved his operation to the high-tech plant at Wapping. Prior to Murdoch's stand, the unions had held the industry to ransom in various ways and so-called 'Spanish customs' cost firms millions in illicit payments. Spanish customs involved the blatant use of false names such as Mickey Mouse, Donald Duck and, would you believe, Sir Gordon Richards of Tattenham Corner, to secure extra pay packets for union members.

None of this justifies what Piggott did, but it helps to put his crime into perspective. If others had been doing similar things for years, to the knowledge of almost everyone in the racing industry, he would have needed to be a saint not to reap those benefits, too. To adopt a high moral tone over Piggott's unfortunate downfall seems absurd. Brough Scott gave a commendably balanced view when he wrote in the *Sunday Times*: 'Friday's sentence was no doubt correct because we live in a tamed, interdependent world where non-acceptance can lead to anarchy. Lester was a wild animal, answerable to no one. Now we've locked him up. That's sad, for while it's proven how much he took, no one will ever assess how much he gave.'

There, as learned counsel might say, Piggott's case must rest.

CHAPTER EIGHT
A LICENCE TO THRILL

So Piggott swapped his jet-set lifestyle for the mind-numbing and ignominious existence of a gaolbird. Some of those who knew him feared he would crack up under the strain; others felt that he would cope with it, as he did so many other reverses in his life, with the usual stoicism. Suffice it to say at this point that the British penal system did no more to break Lester's spirit than the Stewards of the Jockey Club did thirty years earlier.

Lester began prison life in Norwich gaol, but he spent only four days there. He was detained in the hospital wing and the governor, Andrew Barclay, denied allegations that Piggott was receiving special treatment, the first of many accusations that he was given an easy ride inside.

Three days after the trial, Susan Piggott, who had been granted a temporary training licence when Lester relinquished his own following the verdict, saddled her first winner when Turbine Blade whizzed home in the 4.00 at Nottingham. Tony Ives, the winning rider, said: 'This one's for Lester.'

Two days later Piggott was transferred to Highpoint Prison, a more liberal open gaol near Haverhill. Highpoint, a former RAF station, had been opened ten years previously for low-risk inmates. Allegations of soft treatment surfaced again and there were denials that Piggott would be allowed hampers and champagne for Christmas. He must still have been haunted by memories of the previous year, when he had been arrested a week before the festivities and not long afterwards his mother Iris had died, aged eighty-one.

Piggott shared a well-appointed room with one other prisoner in Highpoint and he had his own toilet. Often there were four prisoners to a cell and Piggott's arrangement caused some resentment. He was also moved quickly into a job in the laundry department, regarded as a cushy number. Furthermore, he was given his release date – exactly a year later – within hours of his arrival at Highpoint. Clearly, therefore, he did receive some concessions, although the picture of his prison life as portrayed on *Spitting Image* was well wide of the mark. One programme showed a grovelling butler fawning over him and asking 'How do you find the going, Lester?' The reply came: 'Very soft, thank you.'

Golf and watching television took up most of his leisure time and there was

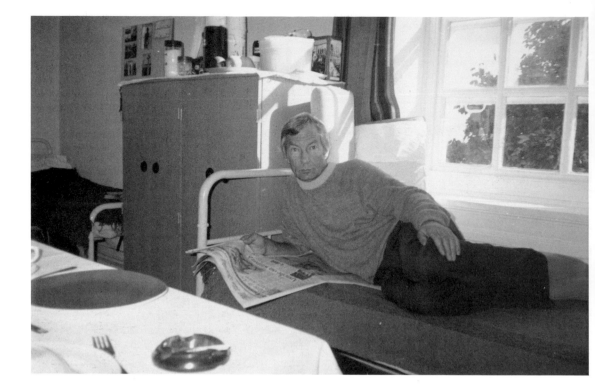

great concern when he collapsed after a game of badminton after being accidentally hit on the head with a racket. The blow, plus the fact that he was eating even less than usual because he did not like the food, caused him to black out; the incident was blown out of all proportion by the media.

Whether he received special treatment or not, Lester soon won the respect of his fellow prisoners. He never moaned about anything, kept his mouth shut and got on with it. He made a lot of friends at Highpoint and maintained secret contact with some of them after he was released. Inevitably he was pestered for racing tips, but he never gave any, at least not to the inmates. However, on 2 June 1988, the *Sun* carried the headline 'Lester Wins 10th Derby from Prison Cell'. The story behind that tenth 'triumph' was that Ray Cochrane had sought Piggott's advice before riding Kahyasi to victory in the Blue Riband.

Cochrane asked Susan Piggott if she would ask Lester the best way to ride Kahyasi when she visited him in prison. Cochrane was concerned about being drawn thirteen of fourteen. Lester told Cochrane 'Let Kahyasi flow along with the pack, then take a position from the top of the hill.' Cochrane, who not many years previously had almost quit the game because of weight and injury problems, carried out Piggott's battle-plan to perfection and punched the air ecstatically as he sailed home to his first Derby triumph. 'Without Lester this Derby would never have happened,' he said.

ABOVE Family man: Piggott relaxes with daughters Tracy (left) and Maureen, and wife Susan. During his stay in prison he gave advice to Tracy before she rode her first winner in Ireland

RIGHT Susan Piggott aboard her pony Pepe on Newmarket Heath. She received serious injuries when Pepe threw her during Lester's time in Highpoint

OPPOSITE Bed and bored: Piggott, seen here reading the *Sporting Life* in his cell at Highpoint Prison, found boredom the worst aspect of his year in prison

Two months later, Piggott also helped his daughter Tracy to a memorable success. Tracy, then aged twenty-two, won her first race, on Husaam at Leopardstown, and said 'I talked to Dad on the phone during the week and he told me Leopardstown was one of his favourite tracks and gave me advice on how to ride my horse.'

Meanwhile, life was becoming more and more miserable for Lester, although his suffering had nothing to do with prison conditions. Five days after the Derby Piggott was stripped of the OBE he had been awarded in 1975 for his services to racing. His tax dodging had already cost him a knighthood and friends said that few things in life hurt him as deeply as the withdrawal of his OBE. A few weeks later, Piggott's father, Keith, suffered a bad heart attack; Lester was allowed out of prison to visit him. Worse was to come one week later when Susan went into a coma after suffering a horrendous fall while riding her pony, Pepe, on Newmarket Heath. So bad were her injuries – a double fracture of the skull, ten broken ribs and a broken collarbone – that there were real fears that she might not pull through. She went into intensive care in Addenbrooke's Hospital in Cambridge where she was sedated with powerful drugs to keep her immobile and ease the acute pain. Because of the sedation she was put on a ventilator to assist her breathing.

A week after Susan's fall, Lester was allowed out of jail to visit her. Ashen-faced and unshaven, Piggott spent forty minutes at Susan's bedside and staff were touched when he leant down to gently plant a kiss on her forehead. Perhaps Lester's touch worked its magic again because Susan made far faster progress than expected and just three weeks later she was discharged and driven home by her daughter Maureen, who had discovered her prostrate body on the Heath a month previously.

Five weeks later, on 24 October 1988, Maureen was entrusted with the joyous task of driving her father home from prison after Douglas Hurd, the Home Secretary, had officially sanctioned Piggott's release. Mayhem surrounded Eve Lodge as the media circus fought for the first pictures of Lester's homecoming and although he consented to pose – even to smile – for the cameras with Susan and the little villain, Pepe, he had some harsh words for the press, who, he said, had made his stay in prison far harder to endure because of the absurd and untrue stories that had been circulating.

A few days later, Geoff and Trish Wragg organised a small birthday party for Lester at the Hole in the Wall restaurant in Cambridge. 'We hadn't seen him for a year, but it was as if he'd never been away. He didn't seem any different,' Wragg says. Others noticed subtle changes, however. Charles St George said: 'After coming out of gaol, Lester was like a man who has been through a serious illness. He was far more relaxed and never worried about anything any more, even money. He talked very little about prison and when he did he only told you the funny things. He would never say "God, I was desperate in there."' The only

It's great to be back: The anticipation shows on Piggott's face as he bursts from the stalls at Leicester in October 1990 on his first day back since his retirement (Gerry Cranham)

ABOVE That's magic! Less than a fortnight after making his comeback at the age of fifty-four, Piggott produces a sensational finish to take the Breeders' Cup Mile at Belmont Park on Royal Academy and (right) he enjoys the re-run even more (All-Sport/Trevor Jones)

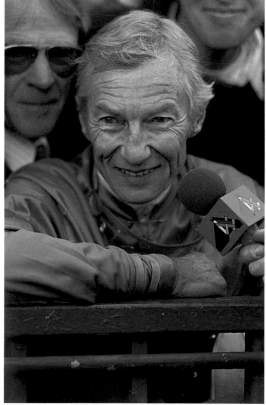

OPPOSITE Piggott riding Lupescu is nosed out by young Gary Carter on Sumonda at Leicester on his first ride back, but (left) he savours that winning feeling again the following day after booting home a double at Chepstow (George Selwyn/All-Sport)

ABOVE Keeping it in the family: Piggott comes home to win the 1991 Greenham Stakes at Newbury on Bog Trotter, trained by his son-in-law, William Haggas. The colt proved a dismal failure in the 2,000 Guineas (Gerry Cranham)

RIGHT The old firm back in business: Piggott, Vincent O'Brien (hat) and Robert Sangster together again before the 1991 Irish Derby (Gerry Cranham)

OPPOSITE A beaming Piggott escorts his daughter, Maureen, to the church for her wedding to Newmarket trainer, William Haggas, in March 1989 (Trevor Jones)

ABOVE Getting it off Pat: Piggott brings Mudaffar through from a seemingly impossible position to inch out Pat Eddery on Troupe at the Doncaster St Leger meeting of 1991 (Gerry Cranham)

LEFT I did it his way: Alan Munro takes advice from the master before riding Generous to victory in the 1991 Irish Derby at The Curragh (Gerry Cranham)

OPPOSITE Seeing is believing as fifty-six-year-old Piggott pounces aboard Rodrigo de Triano to notch up Classic win number thirty in the 1992 2,000 Guineas. And (right) they swoop for further glory in the Irish Guineas a fortnight later (Trevor Jones/All-Sport)

Prize guy: Piggott shows his delight after being voted Personality of the Year by his colleagues at the first Jockeys' Awards ceremony in 1991. The awards have since become known as 'The Lesters' (Trevor Jones)

significant comment about jail that Lester made to various friends was that it was 'A f—g waste of time!' Few could have treated such a demeaning experience with such extraordinary indifference.

Just over four months after his release, on 4 March 1989, the cameras captured Lester and Maureen at an even happier moment. The venue was St Martin's Church at Exning and the occasion was Maureen's wedding to the young Newmarket trainer William Haggas, which had been postponed because of Lester's imprisonment. Tracy was one of the bridesmaids and another young Newmarket trainer, William Jarvis, was best man. The guests included Henry Cooper and Charles St George.

Maureen, looking radiant in a full-length white silk dress and carrying a bouquet of lilies of the valley, arrived ten minutes late on Lester's arm. Lester, who was to become a grandfather at the end of the year when Maureen gave birth to a daughter, looked splendidly elegant in grey morning suit, but smiled somewhat self-consciously and gave the impression that he might feel more comfortable facing the Stewards of the Jockey Club.

At this point Lester cannot have been feeling too badly disposed towards the august men of Portman Square, because shortly before he left prison they had decided not to heap further misery on him. After Piggott's conviction, Peter Twite, head of the Jockey Club's administration department, had broached the question of whether Piggott would be liable to a further punishment from the sport's administrators by saying: 'This is an unusual case. The question is whether it is an offence in relation to racing. I'm not sure that it is. It is a financial matter. He has received his money out of racing, but whether or not that could create an offence under racing rules is not clear.' Some five weeks before he was released a Jockey Club statement said that Piggott would not be punished for 'bringing the sport into disrepute'. The statement said: 'The evidence produced at his trial indicates that Lester Piggott may have committed acts liable to cause serious damage to the interests of racing which would be a breach of rule 220 (iii) as it stood at the time.' But it went on: 'Taking into account the fact that he is, in effect, already serving a period of disqualification by being imprisoned for a tax offence, and mindful of his past services to racing, the Stewards have decided to take no further action in the matter.'

The stewards also decided they would take no action over the allegations of betting levelled at Piggott as there was insufficient evidence to warrant holding an inquiry. But the most significant paragraph of their statement read: 'Should Lester Piggott make an application for a licence to train, it will be considered by the Licensing Committee in the light of all the facts available at the time.' Not totally positive, perhaps, but those few words had opened the way for Piggott's return not just to racing, but to a position of respectability in the business he lived and breathed. The exact form that return would eventually take could not have been envisaged by even his most obsessive supporter.

For almost two years after his release we saw very little of Lester. He was said to be getting increasingly depressed as he maintained a low profile pootling about behind the scenes helping Susan, who retained the training licence in her name. Then, not for the first time in his life, he suddenly turned the world of racing upside down.

At about 5.30 pm on the afternoon of 11 October 1990, Piggott walked out of the Jockey Club headquarters clutching what was to become arguably the most talked-about piece of paper since Neville Chamberlain stepped off a plane in September, 1938 waving Adolph Hitler's signature in front of him and proclaiming 'I believe it is peace in our time'. The office workers and shoppers rushing for buses and trains in the chaos of a West End rush hour would hardly have given the gaunt, grey-haired grandfather a second glance as he emerged into the chill of an autumn evening. Yet within the hour his face would be seen by millions on national television news. The next morning the stunning implication of his mission to Portman Square would scream out to the world from newspaper headlines.

'Lester Rides Again', the front page of the *Sporting Life* proclaimed. 'Lester's Back!' the *Racing Post* trumpeted. Now the full significance of the small buff document that Piggott had been holding in his hand became clear. Headed 'Rules of Racing – Jockey's Licence', it was the introductory page to the latest and most improbable chapter in the extraordinary life of Lester Keith Piggott.

In truth, the seeds of Piggott's return to the saddle had been sown the day he hung up his riding boots. If others rode to live, Lester lived to ride. Retiring from the saddle was something he felt he *ought* to do; he had no great yearning to train. It is clear that Susan was heavily behind what was to prove in personal terms the most unsatisfactory decision of Lester's life.

There was no doubt in most people's minds that Piggott's unique empathy with horses would enable him to make it to the top as a trainer. And in the short time he held a licence at his Eve Lodge yard on Newmarket's Hamilton Road he had already gone a long way towards proving it. In his first season in 1986 he sent out thirty winners in Britain, including a Royal Ascot triumph with Cutting Blade. During the 1987 campaign his heart was clearly not in the game with the trial looming over him, but among his tally was a first Classic triumph in the Oaks d'Italia with Lady Bentley. Yet whatever heights Piggott might have reached as a trainer he would always have been merely going through the motions. In his new role he was relatively speaking a supporting player, an unfilfilled artisan, as opposed to the thrusting solo artist who seduced his adoring public with extraordinary feats in the saddle.

The slow and painstaking business of preparing Thoroughbreds to race could not remotely compare with riding them. Piggott was purely concerned with the finished article, the moment when the raw recruit had been transformed into a racing machine. He would ride out regularly, but rather than concentrating on the day-to-day working and honing of the horses, which he left to Susan, Lester's role was more that of campaign manager. Entering the horses for races and assessing the opposition at least allowed him to maintain some sort of influence over the business of winning races, which was his raison d'être.

Furthermore, Piggott had been used to a regular association with the absolute cream of racehorses, with owners and trainers falling over themselves to secure his services for their best animals. Working with a team comprised mainly of relatively ordinary horses in his yard was something of a comedown.

Geoff Lewis puts it another way. 'Lester knew the strength of the opposition he was up against – men like Henry Cecil, Michael Stoute and Luca Cumani, who were established masters of their profession. With them standing in his way he realised it would be incredibly difficult to make it to the top as a trainer. And knowing Lester he would have considered himself a failure if had been anything less than number one.'

Nor was Piggott the sort of man to enjoy the obligatory socialising with owners, the public relations exercise that forms such a large part of a trainer's schedule. Immersing himself in the polite chit-chat of the racecourse bar or the dinner table would have been absolute anathema to him. Elegant and at ease though he had looked in grey morning suit when he welcomed back Cutting Blade at Royal Ascot, a meeting he had dominated as a rider, it was easy to discern the discomfort behind the facade. 'Training winners is a lot harder than riding them,' he said in that off-hand way of his after watching Cash Asmussen jump down jauntily from Cutting Blade's back. Those who knew what motivated the man appreciated the full weight of that statement.

Bryn Crossley, who regularly rode for Piggott, remembered how Lester would have a look of sheer yearning in his eyes when he watched Crossley depart for the races from Eve Lodge. 'Lester would come up to me in the yard before I set off to go racing and say something like "You're off to Nottingham today, aren't you? I suppose it'll take you about two hours. You'll be leaving about quarter past eleven then." You could see the envy written all over his face.'

Many will claim that money was the only thing that motivated Lester, but that would be wrong. Race riding in itself was like a drug for him; the withdrawal symptoms were too painful to overcome. Therefore it was hardly surprising that thoughts of securing another 'fix' were never far from his mind. Within just six months of his official retirement – he had continued to make guest appearances round the world for several weeks – plans for Piggott's return were already being put into operation. In April 1986 he had been booked to ride Robert Sangster's Tate Gallery in the 2,000 Guineas after Vincent O'Brien's stable jockey, Pat Eddery, had received a suspension that ruled him out of the race. Piggott had been over to Ballydoyle to work Tate Gallery a couple of weeks before the Guineas and when his comeback was announced Ben Hanbury, the Newmarket trainer, was quick to snap him up for his 1,000 Guineas candidate, Midway Lady, ridden

Lester explains what life is like on the other side of the track when he is interviewed as a trainer on Derby day

to victory by Piggott in important juvenile events in England and France the previous autumn.

Two days later it all came crashing down around him. Contractual arrangements with firms who had manufactured commemorative items based on Piggott's retirement, such as a limited edition of 2,000 Royal Worcester plates, could not be broken; and that meant Piggott's riding boots back in mothballs, Lester himself condemned indefinitely to his new life of rampant boredom. Or so it seemed; but the way back had not been closed for ever. Piggott had to wait three and a half years, one of which was spent languishing in prison, before a phone call from his old friend, Charles St George, one December morning in 1989 set the wheels of his return inexorably in motion. Those first steps towards Piggott's professional resurrection were taken in – of all places – Peru. Following a visit to Newmarket, Juan Thorne, a Peruvian racing official and racehorse owner and friend of the St Georges, had arranged for Walter Swinburn to ride one of his horses in the Lima Gold Cup. Swinburn phoned St George's son, David, who was organising the trip, shortly before they were due to leave and said that he would not be able to go because of illness. 'I said to Dad, "Why not ask Lester?" David recalled. "He did and amazingly Lester accepted. Lester took the trip very seriously and was particularly careful about his weight. He hardly ate at all during the whole trip.'

But if Piggott took the business of getting back on the track seriously, albeit at an obscure Peruvian venue, he certainly did not play it entirely straight. 'Although Lester is my godfather, I had never really got to know him well up to then,' David explains. 'Travelling with the great man for a week was a fantastic experience for me. I had heard abut Lester's wicked sense of humour and I experienced it first hand.'

The journey did not begin too propitiously as they missed their connection at Frankfurt due to mistiming by Lufthansa. After Lester had loosed off a few choice Anglo-Saxon words at the German officials they then embarked on an exhausting 36-hour series of flights via Caracas and Bogotá to Lima, during which time Lester's good humour returned.

'Our host had sent us first-class tickets, but on one leg of our journey they put us in the economy section with an old South American lady sitting between us,' David recalls. 'She spilt oil from her meal on her clothes and let out a scream. She was babbling away to Lester in Spanish, presumably asking him to do something. He just nodded very seriously and pretended to take it all in.

'Then when they handed out the landing cards she was having difficulty filling hers in. Lester offered to fill it in for her. He took her glasses off her face and put them on and began scribbling away. When he had finished I saw that he had written a load of absolute balls, putting down things like "Church of England" in the section marked "Sex".'

Piggott found the real business of the visit no laughing matter. Eight thousand fans turned out at Lima's Monterrico racetrack – hardly Royal Ascot – to watch

A different sort of horse power for Piggott as he enjoys a day away from the track

him ride competitively for the first time in almost four years. His best placing was a third on Sulieman and he finished plum last on his two other rides. The pay cheque of $20 he received for finishing third on Sulieman was surely his smallest ever. He donated it to a local Mutualista fund. But the Peruvians hardly noticed that Piggott had failed to win; his mere presence was sufficient reason for a carnival. They feted him like a head of state and afterwards an offical presented him with a silver tray inscribed 'Maximum Jockey'.

It was seven months before Piggott took the next significant step along the road back. In July 1990 he brought the Irish flocking in as if they were handing out free Murphy's all round when he rode in an invitation race at Tipperary and a veterans' race at the Curragh two days later.

Jonjo O'Neill, the laughing cavalier who so enlivened the English jumping scene in the eighties, spoiled Piggott's party at Tipperary. Riding Allegoric, O'Neill beat Piggott on Don Leone by a length and a half. Piggott, blowing heavily, said: 'It was hard work out there.' Lester's ride on Legal Legend in the Curragh veterans' race proved even less successful – he was beaten into third place behind former French champion, Yves Saint-Martin, riding Chirkpar – yet it was far more noteworthy for one reason: Legal Legend was trained by none other than Vincent O'Brien. If only for one fleeting moment, the most celebrated partnership in modern racing was back together again.

Piggott, as monosyllabic as ever, played down rumours of a serious comeback, saying: 'I don't think it's on.' O'Brien, however, saw it differently. The canny Irishman is almost as good a judge of humans as he is of horses, so, having sensed the frustration gnawing away at Piggott through those unfulfilling years and seeing now the light of battle returning to his eyes, O'Brien set to work in that inimitably gentle way of his to persuade his old friend to go the whole hog.

That's Racing, a recent collection of racing memories, contains a short piece on Lester by O'Brien in which he wrote: 'When Lester set up as a trainer I felt it was not what really interested him. Yet, I had known Susan, a daughter of Sam Armstrong, as a young girl . . . and seen her instructing young apprentices in her father's yard. I felt that training was bred in her bones.

'In July 1990 my son-in-law John Magnier told me that he had met Lester recently and asked him how he spent his days. Lester said he rode out in the mornings and watched racing on SIS [satellite television] in the afternoons. John said: "Why don't you start race riding again?" and added "You think about it." I rang Lester in August and said what John had told me and how about it? He said: "I'll give it some thought."'

So it was that the seed began to germinate in Lester's mind. The buzz of riding in a race again, albeit it strictly a novelty affair, had stirred his senses beyond the point of no return. Now, every time he rode out for Susan on misty mornings on the Heath he visualised himself pulling on racing silks again, imagining the prospect of launching those keyed-up Thoroughbreds into overdrive instead of merely confining himself to second gear.

Piggott met O'Brien in Dublin in September and told him he had decided that he would ride again. For some while he talked constantly to Susan about making a return. Eventually, she said to him: 'Instead of just talking about it, why don't you just go out and do it.' Within forty-eight hours he had; and though racing's grapevine is probably more adept at ferreting out secrets than MI5, Piggott's decision came as a bombshell even to many of his closest friends.

Having been approached by Piggott just two days before, the Jockey Club slotted him into one of their licensing sessions on Thursday 11 October. Piggott was examined by the Jockey Club's doctor, Michael Allen, prior to the meeting and found to be in exceptional health, with the blood pressure of a young man. 'If you train your body and maintain a regimen like Lester you never lose your fitness. He has always been and still is a superb athlete,' Dr Allen says.

After an interview lasting some thirty minutes, Piggott was handed his licence and went upstairs with David Pipe, the Club's director of public affairs, to prepare a brief statement to be issued to the media. 'Lester didn't say much and he didn't exactly seem over the moon,' Pipe recalls. Another aspect of Lester that clearly hadn't changed a bit. He was, however, more expansive in an interview with the *Sporting Life* shortly afterwards. 'I suppose it is true to say that I was bored after riding out in the mornings because we haven't got all that many horses at the moment,' he explained. 'Lots of people have been asking me why, but my only answer to that is "why not?" I feel in such good shape that it is worth giving it a try. I wouldn't be doing it if I didn't think there were opportunities for me and that I could do myself justice. I am not out to make a fool of myself.'

The immediate reaction of many people when the news broke was that someone was trying to make a fool of them and that the whole thing was a giant leg-pull, especially when a putative appearance in Europe's richest juvenile event, the Cartier Million in Ireland the next day, came to nothing. However, the following Monday the 'hoax' became reality. 'Leicester Piggott' one headline read, relaying the news that Lester would be back in the flesh at the midlands course for three rides that afternoon.

Lowly Leicester, like Nottingham almost five years previously, had never seen anything like it. One thing the assembled masses did not witness, however, was a side of Piggott few if any knew existed. The man who had always appeared not to have a single nerve in his body, who had steered nine Derby winners home in front of a quarter of a million people on Epsom Downs as if he were riding in a penny-ante affair at Pontefract, was suddenly as nervous as a schoolkid waiting outside the headmaster's study. Bryn Crossley, who had driven Piggott to Leicester, recalls: 'Amazingly, no one spotted us arriving and when we parked the car Lester just sat there for a while without saying anything. I could see he was tense, so I asked him if he was okay. He just grunted, then after a while he said "Where are they all?" Once he saw the hordes of people coming towards him he relaxed.'

As Lester ran the gauntlet of backslappers and the cameras clicked and whirred, Britain's betting shops were crammed as full as rush-hour tube trains with punters straining incredulously to watch their hero's return on satellite TV. Bookmakers offered special Piggott bets, including odds of 100–1 against him for the 1991 jockeys' championship.

David Johnson, a clergyman from nearby Lutterworth, turned up at his local course especially to see Piggott. 'People say Lester is a scoundrel, but I respect him for his professionalism,' Johnson told the *Racing Post*. 'I cannot ride a horse and I'm sure Lester cannot preach a sermon, but I admire him for the way he goes about his job.'

Not only the public made clear their unique affection for Piggott; so too did his colleagues, who gave him a standing ovation when he walked into the weighing room. Many jockeys booked rides at Leicester especially so they could be there

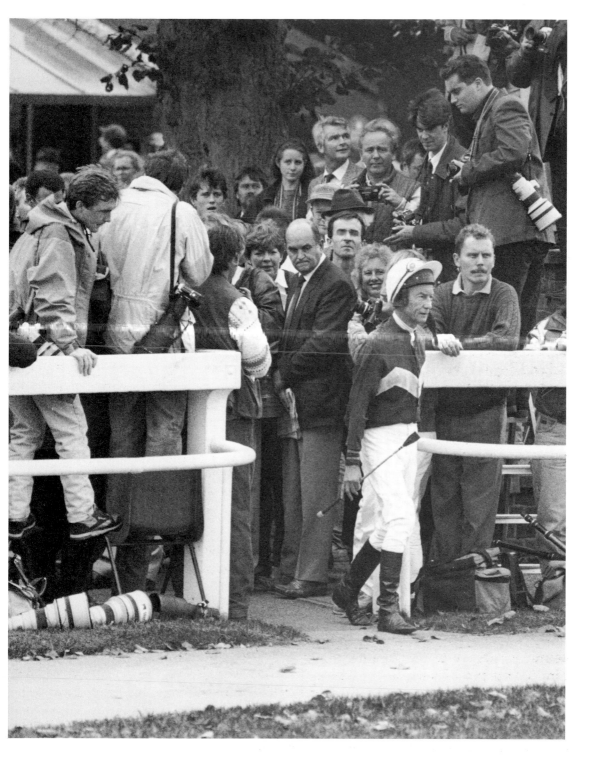

Back in the old routine: Piggott walks back into racing at Leicester after a five-year absence

for his return and some continued to follow the Piggott circus around for some while just to be part of the celebration while it lasted.

But was that all it was to be – just a circus? Many feared that it could not possibly amount to anything more. At fifty-four going on fifty-five, Piggott was by no means the oldest jockey to ride; in recent years Alec Russell had gone on until he was fifty-seven and the amazing little American, Bill Shoemaker, had given up only at fifty-eight, nine months before Piggott's return, having ridden a world record 8,883 winners. Several have even gone on into their sixties, notably Frank Buckle, whose record of twenty-seven Classic winners was eclipsed by Piggott and who went on to sixty-five; but the ultimate Methuselah of the saddle was Harry Beasley, who won the 1891 Grand National on Come Away, and had his last mount at the age of eighty-three.

The difference with Piggott, however, was the weighty matter of a five-year break from the saddle, with a year of incarceration thrown in. Everyone naturally hoped that he would return with his genius fully intact, but few believed he could possibly do so and many suspected it would end in disaster.

Jimmy Lindley, one of Piggott's most successful contemporaries and now a member of the BBC commentary team, said: 'I doubt whether Lester can really turn back the years. A champion can never regain his crown. The main problem for him will be getting his brain to react as quickly as it used to. You have to think ten times quicker in a race. It's like riding a motorbike at a hundred miles an hour.'

Willie Carson, the five times champion jockey, then enjoying a scorching Indian summer to his career, made a plea to Piggott to give up the idea of a comeback altogether. In an article by Nigel Clarke in the *Daily Mirror*, Carson was quoted as saying, 'We all wish Lester the best of luck, but I'm worried for him. It will be very hard for him after five years out of the game. We don't want Lester coming back a mere shadow of his former self. He was a real legend and we don't want the memory to fade.'

What Lindley and Carson said had made sense and summed up the feelings of a broad cross-section of opinion. Yet there were those, notably Shoemaker, who felt Piggott could not be assessed by conventional wisdom.

'I would say that for the average guy of fifty-five years old it would be very tough to make a comeback,' Shoemaker said. 'But Lester Piggott is not an average kind of guy. He's unique, so there's no reason why he shouldn't do it. I'm sure he'll be very successful for the next five years if he wants to be.'

Finally, after all the words and all the hype, the reality arrived – Leicester Piggott day was upon us. For his first ride back Lester donned the famous black and white colours of Charles St George on Lupescu and watching him fail by only the width of one of his famous cigars after a titanic struggle with young Gary Carter on Sumonda (Piggott had already ridden three Derby winners when Carter was born) it really did seem as if he had never been away.

The long and the short of it. Piggott with Willie Shoemaker, the prolific American rider, who was one of the few people to express faith in Piggott's ability to make a successful comeback

'It didn't feel any different. I'm doing the same as ever – one leg each side,' Piggott said. 'I've had no trouble with my weight, I only had to miss Sunday lunch. But I'm bound to need a race or two to get back to my best.'

Within twenty-four hours Piggott was back in the winner's enclosure, across the Welsh border in Chepstow. Demonstrating all the nonchalance and consummate judgement that had characterised his halcyon days, he surged home first on Nicholas, trained fittingly by his wife. Half an hour later he made it a double with an equally polished performance on Shining Jewel. Lord Hartington, the Senior Steward of the Jockey Club, was among the ecstatic fans at the Welsh track and seemed as moved as anyone by Piggott's rebirth. 'It's fantastic. There are some wonderful people in racing with whom the public can identify and Lester ranks among the highest of these,' Hartington proclaimed. 'We are lucky to have him around.'

And so said all of us, particularly when the next few days produced more reminders of that old Lester magic. A first comeback winner in England on Chimayo at Newmarket was followed by a winning spree at the Curragh which enabled Piggott to upstage Pat Eddery in one of his finest hours. Eddery, on his way to an eighth jockeys' title, became the first man since Sir Gordon Richards in 1952 (the year of Eddery's birth) to ride 200 winners in a season when he booted home Miranda Jay at Chepstow. The same afternoon Piggott weighed in with four winners for Vincent O'Brien at The Curragh. Only he could have stolen Eddery's thunder in such a way. 'It was like having a Derby winner. The public are having a great day, aren't they?' O'Brien said.

The public and the whole racing world were indeed having an unforgettable time as Piggott conjured up visions of the past. The week had been almost beyond belief. Yet four days later it was to be eclipsed by the overpowering drama that took place in the emotion-charged atmosphere of a New York afternoon.

CHAPTER NINE
BEDLAM IN THE BIG APPLE

The Americans certainly know how to put on a show, which is why within a few years of its inception in 1984 the Breeders' Cup had already become a sporting institution. Other nations could only look on in envy as year after year the seven-race extravaganza, with its $10 million in purses, dished up a feast of entertainment. The build-up and the razzmatazz create an atmosphere that transcends the sport and many of the championship races themselves are epics. Who could forget the surge of the great Alysheba in the $3 million Breeders' Cup Classic at Churchill Downs in Kentucky in 1988, when the brilliant colt sped across the wire in the gathering gloom, illuminated by the glow of a thousand flash bulbs, to become the greatest money winner of all time? And on the same afternoon the sustained duel between two queens of the track in the $1 million Distaff mesmerised a watching nation as Personal Ensign, who was racing with five screws in her left leg, wore down the Kentucky Derby heroine Winning Colors to end a remarkable twelve-race career undefeated.

A year later the pre-race publicity surrounding the Classic confrontation between old rivals Sunday Silence and Easy Goer at Gulfstream Park in Florida reached the sort of proportions that would usually be expected for an Ali–Frazier fight or a Super Bowl clash between the San Francisco 49ers and the Buffalo Bills.

Compulsive viewing was what the fans had come to expect, yet as over 51,000 people poured through the gates of Belmont Park's ivy-clad grandstand on that Saturday in October 1990, none of them could have envisaged the amazing scenes they were about to witness. Nothing any Hollywood scriptwriter could have dreamed up would have compared to the sustained drama that was set before them on that chilly afternoon in the cosmopolitan surroundings of New York's Jamaica district.

For Brits and native New Yorkers alive, Breeders' Cup day 1990 would be remembered as the day Lester Piggott returned to rock the Big Apple to its core. Yet there was so much more to those few hours of heart-stopping action that the mind could hardly take it all in. It was an afternoon that would be talked about for years to come and many seasoned racegoers were to describe it as the most extraordinary day's racing there had ever been.

American dream: Jacqueline O'Brien greets Piggott and Royal Academy after their story-book triumph in the Breeders' Cup in New York in 1990

For the vast contingent of British racing enthusiasts who made the trip to New York and the millions watching on television back in Blighty, Breeders' Cup 1990 offered real promise of ending the frustrating drought that had seen Britain's transatlantic task force return empty-handed every year since the great mare, Pebbles, galloped off with the 1985 Turf to become our first Cup winner. British runners had often been disadvantaged by local weather conditions and the tight American tracks, but conditions at Belmont Park provided them with no excuses. Temperatures under a clear blue sky were in the low forties and the wide Belmont circuit, with its broad, sweeping turns, looked a breeze even for the most ungainly of gallopers.

According to bookies and pundits alike, by far the best chance of a British success lay with the lightning-fast Dayjur, trained from his wheelchair by Major Dick Hern, who had hauled himself back to the top after the most appalling adversity in his professional and personal life. Not even the combination of a crippling hunting accident and the summary and controversial termination by the Queen of the lease of his Berkshire stables could keep the indomitable Major Hern down for long, and now he was set to conquer new horizons in the Indian summer of a remarkable career. Rated the best sprinter for years after a succession of brilliant wins in England, Dayjur looked an awesome talent, yet even those who prophesied his success did not deny that he was up against it. Taking on the American sprinters in their own backyard had up to then been considered mission impossible.

The $1 million Sprint led off the proceedings and within seconds of the stalls bursting open the crowd were gasping in horror. Racing helter-skelter for the turn, Mr Nickerson, one of the leading US contenders, collapsed from a fatal heart attack, bringing down Shaker Knit. Chris Antley, Mr Nickerson's rider, escaped from the melee of flying hooves with a broken collarbone. José Santos, who was tossed into the air like a rag doll when Shaker Knit ran into his prone rival, had an even more miraculous escape, emerging virtually unscathed and going on to win the Juvenile Fillies on Meadow Star half an hour later.

Meanwhile, English supporters were already in a frenzy as Dayjur scorched into the stretch with only the home-trained filly, Safely Kept, able to keep pace with him. Safely Kept matched Dayjur stride for stride as they duelled clear of the pack, but it was soon obvious that Willie Carson, punching Dayjur out with hands and heels, had his rival cooked. Inside the last furlong Dayjur gradually edged ahead. A hundred yards from the wire he was half a length up and sailing home to a fantastic triumph – until he suddenly precipitated one of the most bizarre incidents in modern Turf history. The sunlit grandstand had cast giant shadows across the track and it was one of these, from the timer's booth, that suddenly fazed Dayjur. Attempting to jump the shadow, he leapt into the air before sprawling back onto the dirt and handing the race to an astonished Craig Perret on Safely Kept. Dayjur rallied gamely but it was too late to close the gap; and then, incredibly, he jumped another shadow right on the line.

An hour later, with the crowd still buzzing from that cataclysmic curtain-raiser, there was shock of a far more sickening kind in the meeting between two outstanding female talents, Go For Wand and Bayakoa, in the Distaff. It was a confrontation that had the cognoscenti drooling – the irresistible force against the immovable object. Go For Wand, the locally trained three-year-old, had won her previous five starts and was sent off as favourite by the New York horse players, who would not hear of defeat even though she was up against a proven champion in the Argentine-bred six-year-old Bayakoa, winner of twenty races, including the previous year's Distaff, and over $2 million in prize money.

As it had promised, the race soon resolved itself into a titanic duel. Go For Wand and Bayakoa battled head to head from the start and the withering pace they set left their opponents legless. On and on they galloped with never more than a flaring nostril between them. One of them had to crack; and one did, in a way that made the most hardened onlooker sick to the stomach. At the sixteenth pole, Go For Wand suddenly lurched to her knees, somersaulted and crashed down in a spreadeagled heap in the dirt. She had put her foot in a hole and shattered a fetlock so badly you could see the jagged bone sticking out. Yet through her pain Go For Wand still retained her instinct for victory, and somehow she struggled to her feet and began to lunge for the line.

Billy Badgett, Go For Wand's trainer, the local boy made good, was one of several people who raced across to try to hold the stricken filly down. Badgett, whose horse barn was located no more than a horseshoe's throw away just off the back stretch, had been married just three weeks previously. His wife, Rosemary, who was Go For Wand's exercise rider, cradled the horse's head in her hands before the vet arrived to bring a swift end to her suffering.

Stunned silence enveloped Belmont like a pall. Carl Nafzger, trainer of Kentucky Derby winner Unbridled, whose late thrust denied the English challenger Ibn Bey a glorious win in the Classic at the end of the afternoon, later summed up the mood as Piggott went out to mount Royal Academy before the Mile, just about the time Go For Wand's life was being ended. 'After the tragedy with Go For Wand, the meeting badly needed a lift and the Lester Piggott show gave us just that,' Nafzger said. Perhaps only Lester, the ultimate showman, could have done it. Before the race, though, it seemed as if sentiment might have overtaken logic. Royal Academy was backed down to favourite, but an objective assessment of his chance suggested question marks over the credentials of both horse and rider.

At $3,500,000, the lean and athletic-looking Royal Academy was the most expensive yearling purchased at public auction in 1988. A son of the great Nijinsky, who had carried Piggott to the Triple Crown in 1970, Royal Academy had a mass of winning relatives on his distaff side. His dam, Crimson Saint, had herself won seven of her eleven races in the United States.

History has shown time and again that breeding is a woefully inexact science; the vast sums paid for blue-blooded pedigrees have frequently been money up in smoke. When the Dublin-based Classic Thoroughbreds company invested such a massive sum in Royal Academy their fortunes were at a high point; by the time the colt was boarding the plane for New York just over two years later the company was all but down and out.

Classic Thoroughbreds was launched on the Dublin stock exchange in October 1987, with Royal Academy's trainer, Vincent O'Brien, as chairman. The idea behind the concept was to use O'Brien's reputation as the supreme trainer of racehorses – albeit slightly flagging in recent years – to market the most exclusive racing club. O'Brien had the major stake of just over 12 per cent, while Robert Sangster, his stud supremo, John Magnier, and Michael Smurfit, the millionaire businessman and racehorse owner, took 8 per cent each with John Horgan, a member of the famed racing and punting family from Cork, taking on around 3 per cent. The involvement of these five major players, who between them invested over IR£3 million, persuaded institutional investors to stump up around IR£5 million and the public another IR£2 million. Investors were falling over themselves in the rush to carve a slice of what appeared to be a genuine racing certainty and the issue was oversubscribed four times. When Saratogan, apparently the best of the company's first yearling purchases, put himself forward as a leading candidate for the 1989 2,000 Guineas the shares rose from their launch price of 30p to around 41p.

Saratogan finished only ninth at Newmarket; other Classic standard-bearers such as Classic Fame and Classic Secret also failed to deliver. The O'Brien magic seemed to have disappeared when it was needed most and after a series of costly failures the shares of Classic Thoroughbreds had slumped to 4.5p by the time Royal Academy stepped onto the track at Belmont. There was, as the Americans say, a lot of heavy baggage riding on his shoulders.

When Royal Academy made his racecourse debut just over a year earlier he had certainly looked a cracking good colt, just the sort who might finally restore the O'Brien tradition of excellence. With O'Brien's stable jockey John Reid in the saddle, Royal Academy cruised home by ten lengths from thirteen rivals in the Late Developers Stakes, a maiden race at the Curragh. He was immediately nominated as a runner in the Dewhurst Stakes at Newmarket, a race O'Brien had won seven times in the preceding twenty years and which he had used as a stepping-stone to the English Classics for the cream of his juvenile colts, such as Nijinsky, The Minstrel and El Gran Senor. The word was that Royal Academy could not be beaten and he started even-money favourite to overcome six rivals in a field that was not a vintage one by Dewhurst standards.

Reid held Royal Academy up at the rear and made his move with about two of the seven furlongs left to run. Just when backers were anticipating a slaughter there was painful anti-climax as Royal Academy's brief run petered out with pitiful swiftness. He trailed home sixth, some four lengths behind the winner, Dashing Blade. The O'Brien camp could not believe what they had seen.

Sangster has subsequently shed new light on that momentous flop, adding a dash of intrigue to what had previously seemed another straightforward case of deflated hype. 'Vincent was speechless after the Dewhurst. He thought Royal Academy only had to be pointed in the right direction to win,' Sangster says. 'Now I look back on it there is a lot to suggest that his poor running that day was suspicious.

'A week before the Dewhurst a bookmaker rang me up at home to tell me to put extra security on Royal Academy as he was going to be doped. I did not take it seriously – it wasn't until the following year that the news of the Doncaster dopings broke – but I rang Vincent and told him anyway, even though the security at Ballydoyle was incredibly tight already. We never found anything wrong with the horse after the Dewhurst, but in hindsight he should have won the race by five lengths, so it certainly makes you wonder what did happen.'

Whatever afflicted him at Newmarket, Royal Academy had shrugged it off by the start of the following season when he followed an easy win in the Tetrarch

Stakes by running the English 2,000 Guineas winner Tirol to a neck in the Irish equivalent. After he had refused to enter the stalls for the St James's Palace Stakes at Royal Ascot in June, it was decided to switch him to sprinting. Sent back to Newmarket for the July Cup, there was no mysterious capitulation this time and he produced a blistering turn of speed to cut down Great Commotion and Rock City. For his next race Royal Academy was pitted against Dayjur in the Ladbroke Sprint Cup. Dayjur started at 2–1 on and won by a length and a half from Royal Academy, but it would have been a very different scenario had O'Brien's colt not been badly baulked at halfway. He was rapidly whittling away Dayjur's lead at the finish, but the post came too soon.

O'Brien had been going to send Royal Academy over to Newmarket for a seven-furlong Group Two race as his next outing, but the colt began to show such sizzling form on the gallops that it was decided that he should go instead for the million-dollar jackpot at Belmont. In a year when there was no outstanding champion in the Breeders' Cup Mile, his form looked good enough to win, but two things swayed some backers off him.

First, he did not truly stay a mile, although the nature of the Belmont circuit would clearly help him, and second there was a suspicion that he was not always putting it all in at the business end of his races. This thought, allied to the memory of his mulish display at Royal Ascot, made you wonder whether he might boil over in the cauldron of Belmont. Reid, who had ridden him in all his races, denies there was a temperament problem. 'Early on in his career he simply lacked confidence and that is why I would never lay into him,' he explains.

An unkind twist of fate prevented Reid from partnering Royal Academy in New York. Three weeks before the Breeders' Cup the Irishman was decanted from the no-hoper Whippet before the start of the Prix de l'Abbaye at Longchamp, the race that precedes the Prix de l'Arc de Triomphe and which that year became the final triumphal conquest for Dayjur en route to the Breeders' Cup. The fall did not look serious, but Reid was unable to partner In The Groove in the Arc and was later found to have broken his collarbone. That meant that he would be just a spectator when Breeders' Cup '90 took place and the prospect did not please him in the least. 'Vincent told me a fortnight before the Breeders' Cup that he had never had Royal Academy so well. He had been absolutely flying on the gallops at Ballydoyle,' Reid recalls. 'Even though he didn't truly stay a mile I felt sure he would get the trip at Belmont and I was confident he would win. I watched the race with very mixed feelings, I can tell you.'

With Reid out of action the mouth-watering prospect of the old firm of Piggott and O'Brien getting together for another major strike immediately loomed as a very real possibility. O'Brien's son Charles, increasingly the power behind the throne, said shortly after Reid's accident: 'Jockeys are falling over themselves to get on the horse. Lester Piggott has not been ruled out of father's calculations yet. It would appear he has lost nothing for being off for so long.'

Yet while many might have seen Piggott as the natural replacement for Reid, especially after Charles O'Brien's statement, there was nothing automatic about it. The major share-holders in Classic Thoroughbreds, seeing Royal Academy's Belmont run as a last-ditch attempt to breathe life into their moribund company, wanted to be absolutely sure they got the best man for the job. There was much discussion about giving the ride to one of the leading American jockeys. Sentiment could not come into it and Piggott had certainly not convinced everyone that he was back to his best. Niggling away at the back of the mind was the feeling that Piggott's comeback, marvellous though it was, had somehow been stage-managed, that his rides were being hand-picked to ensure that the legend was not too badly tarnished.

In the same week that Piggott made his return, Bjorn Borg, the five times Wimbledon champion, had also announced a comeback at the age of thirty-four, six years after he last played competitive tennis in the French Open. Borg's blast from the past lasted about as long as the toast at breakfast time and made you wonder how Lester, with twenty more years on the clock, could possibly be ready for competition at the highest level. Lindley had said that Piggott's reactions could not possibly be what they were and putting him up against world-class younger rivals in a race like the Breeders' Cup seemed rather like hauling Stirling Moss out of retirement to take on Nigel Mansell and Ayrton Senna in a Grand Prix.

Moreover, while Piggott had been given immediate clearance to ride again by the Jockey Club, the French authorities were by no means overawed by the maestro; to them he was just another has-been. They refused to bend their rule which barred jockeys over fifty from receiving a licence. 'Unfortunately, we cannot make an exception for Lester Piggott,' Louis Romanet, the director of the Société d'Encouragement – the French Jockey Club – stated imperiously. Despite two weeks of furious behind-the-scenes diplomacy the issue had still not been resolved at the time of the Breeders' Cup and after being forced to undergo medical tests and produce extensive documentary evidence, a disgusted Piggott said: 'They are messing me about. It is not an example of Common Market cooperation.' Romanet and his colleagues finally opened the doors for Piggott three days after the Breeders' Cup.

Eventually, however, Vincent O'Brien's deep-rooted faith in the man who had ridden nine English Classic winners for him among a host of major triumphs in Europe was allowed to prevail. Six days before the Breeders' Cup it was announced that Lester would ride Royal Academy in the Mile. The news fired the imagination of a generation of race fans who drooled at the prospect of seeing the ultimate Classic team back together. Two days later Piggott repaid a first instalment on his old friend's faith by booting home that fabulous four-timer at the Curragh.

Vincent was unable to make the trip to New York because he had the flu, and

Charles went over to supervise Royal Academy's preparation instead. Speaking at Belmont, Charles said: 'Royal Academy needs switching off and riding from behind and we have got the right man for the job. He needs a confident jockey like Lester and would not have been suited by an American rider.'

Piggott flew out to New York on the Thursday, two days before the Cup. On the Friday morning, clad in blue quilted jacket and bright red cap, he braved the bitter winds that were whistling across the circuit to sit on Royal Academy for the first time ever and breeze him over a mile on the dirt training track. Piggott described him as a lot like Nijinsky, a big horse who was very much on his toes.

O'Brien's wife Jacqueline says: 'I've never seen Lester so dedicated. He had it in his mind that everything was hanging on this for himself and for Vincent. After riding Royal Academy in the gallop he walked the track and spent a lot of time with the horse. He left nothing undone to make victory as certain as possible.'

On that icy morning, Piggott's hypnotic presence lifted the temperature several degrees for the transatlantic visitors at the track. Meanwhile, the man himself was ensuring that the swarming American media were left firmly out in the cold. Piggott has a long memory when he has been unfairly treated and he has never forgotten the way he was rubbished by the US pressmen after winning the Washington International on Sir Ivor when they said he rode like a bum. After all those years, Piggott's contempt for the American press had still not been erased, so when they asked for an interview after he had galloped Royal Academy, he infuriated them by ignoring their request completely. Minutes later the crimson-faced hacks watched him waving regally from the back of his long black Cadillac as it purred past them and sped off through the track gates.

So the great day dawned. Halfway through that harrowing afternoon there was Piggott in the distinctive colours of Classic Thoroughbreds – green with a gold sash and white cap – loping steely-eyed into the parade ring, helmet strap dangling down across his cheek, whip grasped menacingly in his hand ready to be brandished for a final race-winning lunge. As Lester was legged up on to Royal Academy by Charles O'Brien and began to circle slowly round the paddock, which nestles snugly in the shelter of a 200-year-old white pine, the thoughts of a nation were with him. Yet, while Joe Mercer said Piggott was a man you didn't doubt, some of us were wavering. We hoped, we dreamed, but we also wondered whether such a ridiculous fairy tale could possibly come true.

The opening move of the game was not encouraging. As the thirteen runners – which included Markofdistinction from England and Priolo and Lady Winner from France – burst from the stalls Royal Academy ambled out last of all and was already several lengths adrift of the leaders after a furlong. Piggott said: 'He was a bit scared by the gates, but it wasn't a bad thing that he started slowly as they went such a fast pace.' Geoff Lewis believes it was another canny piece of tactical manoeuvering by his old adversary. 'Although Lester has never admitted it, I reckon he deliberately came out of the gates slowly so he could take up a position on the outside,' Lewis says. 'Royal Academy was a moody sort of horse and if he had been up there early and got messed about he might have turned it in.'

Down the back stretch, Piggott gradually began to ease Royal Academy into contention and moved smoothly past half a dozen rivals. Now the race was really humming and Piggott, on the heels of the leaders, was clearly poised to play a leading role. As the field swung into the straight, however, Royal Academy lost his momentum and from moving like a possible winner he was suddenly under pressure to stay with the leading bunch. 'I was going terribly well into the straight and then something happened and he stopped as if he had been shot,' Lester explained. 'He must have put his foot in a hole or seen something which made him hesitate. It took him fifty yards to pick up again.'

As he made the turn on the outside of the pack, Royal Academy was only seventh, at least half a dozen lengths adrift of the pace-setting Expensive Decision; his chance of victory appeared to have slipped away. Then Piggott got down into the drive position and began to ride with all the old demonic fire. The result was pure magic.

'Royal Academy is THUNDERING down the centre of the track,' yelled Tom Durkin, the commentator. Indeed he was, but there were still four rivals ahead of him and four lengths to make up. A furlong out, twenty-year-old Corey Nakatani, a potent new force on the US riding scene, had urged the rank outsider Itsallgreektome into a narrow lead and looked set for Breeders' Cup glory at his first attempt – until Lester's whip came into play.

Six of the maestro's best on Royal Academy's backside sent the colt into overdrive. 'Lester Piggott is FLAILING away at Royal Academy,' Durkin bawled. He was growing more hysterical by the second and who could blame him. With fifty yards to run Piggott was half a length behind Nakatani as Itsallgreektome sped to the wire. Another four strokes from Lester's stick, this time delivered in that inimitable rapid-fire way, propelled him up to the grey and in the final two strides Royal Academy exploded past him.

Nakatani takes up the story. 'I remember it all like it was yesterday. Before the race I went over to Lester and said "Hi, how're you doing." I told him my horse was a longshot, but I thought he had a good shot at winning. Lester just grunted the way he does.

'I thought I was home in the stretch, but Lester rode a hell of a race. The best horse won but Lester had a lot to do with it. He rode one of those incredible finishes I had heard about. To ride in a race like the Breeders' Cup and get beaten by a legend was no disgrace for me. I know he's one of the greatest ever and it's something I'll never forget.'

As the two horses flashed past the post there was still a momentary hiatus. Had Piggott done it? It looked desperately close, but the frenzied reactions of the Royal Academy camp soon indicated that he had got there and the photograph confirmed that Royal Academy had been as much as a neck to the good.

Jacqueline O'Brien ran down the track towards Lester with her arms open wide, almost speechless with joy. Charles O'Brien, looking overcome with the magnitude of it all, managed to blurt out: 'It's incredible, fantastic. When you write the story no one will believe it; it's so amazing.'

Then suddenly Old Stoneface was smiling. The nickname had on occasions in the past seemed well deserved. He had once been described as having a face like a well-kept grave, and on one occasion had apparently rebuked a trainer who suggested he should at least give his ecstatic supporters a smile, saying: 'Why should I? They'd be throwing things at me if I lost.' The truth is that Lester does smile, albeit relatively rarely. The public might have chosen not to notice in the past, but now they could not fail to do so. As Lester rode back to unsaddle with his blue goggles dangling round his neck, his smile would have lit up the whole of New York. That marvellous face, so 'lived-in' that it looks as if it has been inhabited by generations of squatters, creased up into a delightful toothy grin that seemed to last for ever.

Piggott must have been forced to re-live that spine-tingling finish more times than any other race in his life as the media men almost fought among themselves in an effort to snatch a few priceless words from his mouth. Even the spurned American press were totally overwhelmed. And so obviously moved and delighted by it all was Lester that he probably would have gone on talking all night.

'This was one of my greatest triumphs. I didn't really feel it was a special day, just another day, but these sort of days are marvellous. It's fantastic to win a Breeders' Cup race whether you're twenty, thirty, forty or fifty,' Piggott said. 'I had a nice run all the way through, except for when he hesitated on the turn. He won comfortably really. It was only in the last hundred yards that I really had to ride him.'

Meanwhile, the crowd was going berserk. They had just been privileged to witness probably the greatest sporting comeback of all time; and how they roared and thundered their appreciation. Someone in the unsaddling area shouted out 'Three cheers for Lester' and the whole stadium seemed to take up the call. As he walked back along the narrow walkway that led to the jockeys' room people were leaning over the rail, patting him on the back and ruffling his thatch of silvery hair.

Carl Nafzger said: 'Piggott is one of the great athletes of our time, not just in racing but in world sport. Even at fifty-four, when he understands his game as well as he does and has got the skills he has, athleticism will always overcome age.'

Vincent O'Brien summarises that unforgettable day by saying: 'I was very pleased to have encouraged Lester out of retirement and thrilled that he won the Breeders' Cup on Royal Academy. Riding is his life and he is simply too great a jockey to hang up his boots.' And Jacqueline O'Brien says: 'The Breeders' Cup win meant so much for both Lester and Vincent. When I travelled back to Ireland that night I took back with me the massive sheet covered in purple and gold chrysanthemums that they had put over Royal Academy after the race. It was hanging up over the horse's stable when the boys came in the next morning; it was a marvellous moment.'

Back in England racing folk were wearing out the re-wind button on their videos, playing that minute and a half of heart-warming action over and over again and getting choked up with emotion every time. The following day, under the banner headline 'BEDLAM PREVAILS AS VINTAGE PIGGOTT LIFTS ACADEMY HOME' in the *Racing Post*, various racing personalities gave their views of his achievement. These are just four of them.

David Nicholson, leading National Hunt trainer: 'I think it's unbelievable what Lester has done, but then he's the only one who could have done it.'

Julie Cecil, ex-wife of nine times champion Flat trainer Henry and now training in her own right: 'Nothing has given me more pleasure for a very long time. Lester's an absolute star.'

Robert Armstrong, Piggott's brother-in-law and a prominent Flat trainer: 'It was absolutely marvellous, a vintage Piggott ride, the sort you'd have expected to see over the last forty years. Most of the racing world is delighted. I've just been talking to someone in Hong Kong where Lester is very popular and over there they are saying how marvellous it is.'

Barney Curley, renowned Irish trainer and gambler: 'It was like something out of fantasy land, wasn't it? I don't think anyone else would have won on the horse. He's brilliant. No one deserves it more.'

Now we knew Lester was really back. Anyone who still harboured any doubts was either blind or stupid. It was time to sit back and enjoy the second coming of a sporting superman. Every new thrill he provided for us would be the most gloriously unexpected bonus.

The climactic words of Durkin's commentary as Piggott passed the post on Royal Academy were still ringing in our ears days later. 'Royal Academy does it and a LIVING LEGEND returns!' We thought we had seen it all, but for the umpteenth time this remarkable man had proved us wrong. For his latest trick Lester had wiped out five long years at a stroke.

CHAPTER TEN
THE GALLOPING
GRANDFATHER'S MASTERCLASS

For those who had admired Piggott over many years, his second coming offered an unexpected opportunity to savour his unique brand of genius again. But what of those who were too young to have witnessed for themselves the first phase of his career, for example the new generation of jockeys by whom Piggott was regarded as something of a god? Even those who were emerging stars in their own right found the experience of suddenly jousting cheek-by-jowl with a legend quite overwhelming.

Of the new breed, none has more admiration for Lester than Alan Munro, who was voted jockey of the year in 1991 after a magnificent first season as contract rider to Fahd Salman of which the highlight was the performance of the dual Derby winner Generous. 'Lester is the one we all look up to. I think of him as being a great big thick book of wisdom,' Munro says. 'His comeback was awesome. He's got such an aura about him, such a tremendous presence.

'I've had one brilliant year, but when you think he's had thirty that puts it into perspective. He used me a lot when he was training which was obviously a fantastic compliment. I'd been calling him "Sir" and when he started to ride again it took quite a bit of getting used to for me to call him "Lester".

'Lester's a very warm man and he loves helping you. You don't need to ask him, he'll just come up and point something out. Before I won the Derby on Generous I went up to Lester's house and watched old films of him winning the Derby.

'Lester wasn't there but he set it all up and his father, Keith, showed me the films on this amazing old projector which must be worth a fortune. Keith pointed out where Lester was during the race and told me what I should and shouldn't do. That advice was the best advice you could get and it was an essential part of winning the Derby.

'Lester also helped me before the Irish Derby when Generous beat Suave Dancer [subsequent winner of the Prix de l'Arc de Triomphe]. He was riding Sportsworld for Vincent O'Brien and he came over and gave me a few words of good luck as well as some advice on how to approach the race. He told me he thought my horse would act better than Suave Dancer in the soft ground.

'My dream would be to have the same sort of aura as Lester at the end of my career, but of course it would be impossible.'

Darryl Holland, the star apprentice of the 1991 season, takes a similar view. 'Lester is everybody's hero. He's a great man and he'll always be a legend in my mind. He's so good on the big occasion and he was fantastic in the Breeders' Cup. He's shown that you can come back at the highest level and that there's a few more years left in him yet.

'He's got the best racing brain of anybody. I remember sitting in the sauna one day just before his comeback and the other jockeys were talking about him. One of them said: "He's incredible when it comes to knowing how a race was run. He can tell you exactly where you finished and about how every other horse in the race ran. He never misses anything." Some jockeys wouldn't know about any other horse in the race.

'He doesn't usually talk much in the weighing room, but he wandered over to me on one occasion at Warwick and asked me what I thought of the horse he was riding as I'd won on it previously. I found it amazing that a legend like him should ask the opinion of a kid of nineteen.'

Not all the young stars of the saddle were so respectful, however. Lanfranco Dettori, son of the Italian champion Gianfranco who also rode successfully in England, is a great admirer of Lester, but he has an incurable sense of fun and delighted in taking the mickey out of the eleven-times champion, to whom he always refers as Larry. 'Hey, Larry, they're going to stuff you full of paper and put you in a museum,' Dettori would say in his lilting Italian accent. Or, 'Hey, old man, they should have retired you years ago.' Lester would just grin and mumble back: 'What's he on about?'

While the jockeys may have mixed feelings about Lester in certain areas, their respect is unquestioned and he will always be regarded as number one by his colleagues. Michael Caulfield, the secretary of the Jockeys' Association, is in a better position than anyone to sum up Piggott's unique standing among his fellow professionals and he also praises his work for the Association, of which Piggott is a past President and still an active member.

'Lester was one of the founder members of the Association in 1969 and the work he has done for jockeys behind the scenes is invaluable,' Caulfield says. 'He is the most remarkable defender of the faith. He never misses a meeting and is always available. After his comeback he came to look round our new offices at Newbury between the first and fourth races. He was wearing an overcoat over his silks and he chatted to the staff and looked round every room in the building.

'He invited me to his house when he got his licence back,' Caulfield continues. 'It was the first time I'd met him and I was so nervous. I'm a Catholic and it was like having an audience with the Pope. I said congratulations on the Breeders' Cup and he just smiled. He asked how the Association was progressing and about the officials of the Jockey Club. He reminded me of a wise old politician.

'When we held our first Jockeys' Awards ceremony in 1991 it was as if the Messiah had arrived when he walked in. He was given a standing ovation, the atmosphere was incredible.' Lester was voted personality of the year [he received the award again in 1992] and his beaming face as he accepted the prize told of his sheer delight at being honoured by his colleagues. The awards have since become known as the 'Lesters'.

So, in 1991, Lester was back in the old routine. The weighing room focused again on a familiar taciturn figure sitting quietly pursuing his own thoughts, taking in the new faces around him and as ever refusing to be fussed over by anyone. Brian York, one of Lester's valets, says: 'Some jockeys you've got to pamper like a nanny, but Lester hates to be fussed over. He always gets himself ready. It was so good to have him back. Racing went very dead after Lester left. There'll never be another like him.'

Any doubt that Piggott was back to stay was dispelled when he astounded fellow riders by appearing in a brand new pair of black and maroon riding boots. He had apparently worn the previous pair since the days of Sir Ivor and they had been patched up so many times there was hardly any of the original material left. (Robert Armstrong recalls that when Lester was in Hong Kong a few years ago he took his boots to a local bootmaker and asked them to make him a pair exactly the same. When he went to pick them up he found they had made him a pair full of holes.) Complete with shiny new boots, Lester went out to show those young upstarts – and that included Messrs Eddery, Carson and Co. – exactly what real artistry in the saddle was all about. The grandfather looked as sprightly as a teenager, but he paced himself and tended to pick and choose his mounts rather than dash frantically after every possible winner. Nevertheless, in the twelve months after his comeback he notched up 100 winners at home and abroad.

Before the 1991 season began, Piggott had picked up his first suspension since his return, being banned for four days for improper riding at Saint-Cloud on 4 December 1990. On the same day the Aga Khan stunned British racing by announcing the withdrawal of all his horses from the country in protest at the disqualification of his filly, Aliysa, from the 1989 Oaks. Traces of camphor, a banned substance, were found in a dope test, but the Aga took exception to the Jockey Club's methods in handling the affair. In January, Piggott fixed himself up with a ride in the Derby – the Indian version. Vijay Mallya, a leading Indian owner, said: 'I am bringing Lester not only to ride for me, but also so that the Indian public can see one of the all-time greats.'

It was not all plaudits for Piggott, however; there was a dispute over what was to be his first ride in India for twenty-two years. Tony Murray, who died tragically just over a year later, was the victim of a familiar piece of Piggott manoeuvering as Lester went to switch mounts and then decided to go back to his original ride. In the end he finished unplaced on Speedbird, but was mobbed by admirers after winning a six-furlong race on the same card.

Julie Cecil, greets Golan Heights, her first winner as a trainer, after he had been handled with typical Piggott panache to win at Newmarket in the spring of 1991

Before the Turf season began Piggott also rode in Hong Kong and France and had his first experience of all-weather tracks, landing a double at Lingfield. His first success on grass came on Rare Detail, trained by his wife Susan, at Folkestone four days after the start of the new campaign.

There was a personal bonus for Lester when he rode Golan Heights to win at Newmarket in April, giving Julie Cecil her first winner as a trainer since she set up on her own after her divorce from Henry. The victory cemented a relationship that first began back in the fifties when Lester arrived at Warren Place to take up his position as stable jockey to her father, Sir Noel Murless. Julie was just ten years old at the time and away at school, but she was soon to form a warm and enduring friendship with the lanky youth whom she describes as 'a very funny man'. Lester is certainly a bundle of fun after a couple of glasses of champagne and he was said to be absolutely flying at the party that followed Golan Heights' victory.

It was good to see Lester riding winners of any description, but what the world wanted to know was whether the maestro could add to that record tally of twenty-nine Classics wins. He appeared to have set himself up with a major chance in the 2,000 Guineas when he took the Greenham Stakes at Newbury in April, a traditional Guineas trial, on Bog Trotter, trained by his son-in-law William Haggas. Knowing Piggott's past record, however, Haggas was not counting on anything, not even family ties, and said that he was quite prepared to see Piggott switch to another horse before the Guineas if he felt it had a better chance.

The afternoon of Bog Trotter's victory provided a marvellous cameo of the resurrected Lester. Apart from taking the Greenham, he also won the Spring Cup on St Ninian for the Yorkshire trainer Peter Easterby. The two victories provided contrasting examples of the master tactician at work, with an exquisite display of front-running on Bog Trotter and a more restrained but equally dashing success on St Ninian.

Photographers beseiged Lester as he stood in the unsaddling enclosure receiving his trophies and the warmest of receptions from the crowd, who made it quite clear that they would like the Piggott revival to go on for ever. There was an element of sympathy in the ringing applause, too, for they knew that on his tortuous journey from the past the man had been to hell and back – and it showed. The lines on that famous face seemed more deeply etched than ever, the hair more silvery and perhaps a touch thinner. Even Lester could not prevent the most obvious depredations of time. Yet, above all, the spirit was undimmed. He smiled that toothy, slightly self-conscious smile and looked genuinely over-whelmed by all the attention. The joy of being back there among his people was an entirely mutual affair.

The thoughts of the Piggott fan club were now focused on whether Bog Trotter could go on to win the Guineas a fortnight later, and although the colt started only fourth favourite behind Marju at Newmarket there were many shrewd judges who believed Piggott's mount was the real danger to Hamdan Al Maktoum's unbeaten colt. Sadly, Bog Trotter flattered only to deceive, leading for just five furlongs of the mile race before dropping tamely away to finish twelfth behind Mystiko.

Two days earlier, Piggott had ridden the Irish-trained filly Kooyonga into second place behind the brilliant Shadayid in the 1,000 Guineas. He was subsequently to make a rare error of judgement when he deserted Kooyonga in the Irish 1,000 Guineas three weeks later in order to ride Rua d'Oro for Vincent O'Brien, who had given him first pick of his horses for the season. Rua d'Oro looked the winner as Lester cruised up on the outside in the straight, but the filly stopped to nothing and 22-year-old Warren O'Connor burst ahead to steal the glory on Kooyonga on his first Classic ride.

Once the Guineas had been consigned to the record books, all roads as ever led to Epsom and one of the oldest and most debated questions in racing surfaced again after six long years – what would Lester ride in the Derby? In the event there were not too many options open to him, indicating that some things had

Like old times: Piggott and Vincent O'Brien discuss tactics before the 1991 Irish Derby

changed since he had been away. One of the new factors was the increasing trend for wealthy owners to sign up jockeys to ride exclusively their horses, instead of them being contracted to a trainer. Most of the leading riders were involved in such arrangements in 1991. Pat Eddery was retained by Khalid Abdullah, Willie Carson by Hamdan Al Maktoum, Steve Cauthen by Sheikh Mohammed and Alan Munro by Fahd Salman.

Piggott therefore found it impossible to tinker with the team sheet in the Derby as he had done previously. Nevertheless, as you would expect of the master manipulator, he certainly tried. And as the shadow of the Long Fellow loomed over the Epsom scene again it was an anxious time for some of his jittery contemporaries who remembered one of his least endearing characteristics. Had Piggott failed to secure a ride before the big day, as seemed quite possible at one stage, it would have come as no surprise if some of his fellow riders, fearing that they might suddenly have their mount snatched from under them, were seen at the start with their breeches glued to the saddle.

Once again Piggott delights the crowds at Royal Ascot, where he was untouchable for so many years, bringing home Saddler's Hall (above) to win the 1991 King Edward VII Stakes by a wide margin. And (opposite) he tells trainer Sirrell Griffiths what went wrong after finishing unplaced on the Cheltenham Gold Cup winner, Norton's Coin, in the Queen Alexandra Stakes

One of the principal contenders with whom Piggott was linked was the Lingfield Derby Trial winner Corrupt, who started joint favourite for the Epsom Classic with the French colt Toulon. Piggott got to work on Corrupt's owner, Fathi Kalla, a Lebanese businessman, to try to persuade him to ditch Cash Asmussen, who had won on the colt at Lingfield, but Kalla stayed loyal to Asmussen. Neville Callaghan, Corrupt's trainer, explains the situation that he subsequently had cause to regret. 'At the time there seemed no real case for taking Cash off the horse. The years had gone by for Lester and Cash was champion of France and he'd won on Corrupt at Lingfield.

'Ironically, Cash did not give Corrupt the best of rides at Epsom and if Lester had been on him I believe he would have finished second or third instead of only sixth. Lester is *the* Epsom jockey and much as Cash is a good rider, Lester would have had Corrupt in a better position from the start. Charles St George came up to me afterwards and said "You should have had Lester, you know."'

Lester's failure to get on Corrupt, together with the withdrawal of Vincent O'Brien's Sportsworld, who was considered too immature for Epsom, appeared to have closed the door on his reappearance in the race he had made his own. But four days before that all-important first Wednesday in June he provided the spark to ignite a somewhat lacklustre Derby when it was announced that he had been booked to ride Hokusai, until then not a confirmed starter, by St George.

On form Hokusai had no realistic chance, but with Lester on his back it was impossible to dismiss him out of hand. He started at 25–1, but at one point in the straight he looked a contender for a place at least as Piggott brought him through with the familiar exemplary timing and positioning. In the end Hokusai's stamina gave out and he faded into seventh place as Generous surged away from the field. We had seen enough, however, to know that the supreme Epsom artist had not lost one scintilla of his touch.

There was to be no ride for Piggott in the Oaks and what is more he was denied his chance of winning the French equivalent on Caerlina because of the superstition of her Japanese owner, Kaichi Nitta. Piggott had been hampered on Caerlina at the start of the French 1,000 Guineas and Nitta, who was described as 'totally superstitious' by the trainer, Jean de Roualle, decided that because of the bad luck in that race he would switch riders and not make the trip to France. Eric Legrix proved an able deputy for Piggott in the Chantilly Classic.

So it was on to Royal Ascot, the glittering occasion that Piggott had imbued with his special magic over more than three decades. With Eddery, Carson and company snaffling the best of the rides, there seemed little chance of Piggott improving his record of having been top or joint top rider at the meeting eighteen times. Nevertheless, just one more Ascot flourish from the master would have been enough to stir the blood of Royal Enclosure toppers and Silver Ring punters alike and that was exactly what they got.

Riding Saddler's Hall in the King Edward VII Stakes – the race in which he had sustained that notorious six-month suspension thirty-seven years previously – Piggott outfoxed his rivals as he led all the way to scamper home six lengths ahead of his nearest pursuer, Secret Haunt, ridden by Lanfranco Dettori, whose 'old man' teasing of Lester must have come back to haunt the young Italian. The performance left not just the crowd but the colt's trainer, Michael Stoute, in raptures.

'It was very much Lester's idea to make the running,' Stoute said. 'He told me he should have been closer when he was beaten on him at York and said that he wouldn't be hanging about today. The aggressive tactics made all the difference.'

Piggott showed his delight by saying: 'Terrific. There's nothing like it. It was marvellous. It's the best meeting of the year.'

The show rolled on to Glorious Goodwood the following month, where once again there was only a single Piggott winner, but one that stood out as another gem of vintage Lester. Riding Itsagame for the young Epsom trainer Simon Dow,

Piggott came from last to first in little more time than it takes to light one of his cigars and rewarded his supporters with a 20–1 gift. Dow, saddling his first Goodwood winner, said: 'I could hardly give Lester orders. I just suggested he might tuck him in. It's a schoolboy ambition I've had since I was sixteen. He was superlative, in a class of his own.'

There remained only one chance for Piggott to up his English Classic tally to thirty and that was in the St Leger, which he had already won eight times. A few weeks before the Doncaster event, there was a little Swiss bliss to bolster the overseas Classic haul when he rode the German-trained Tao to win the Swiss Derby.

Piggott certainly appeared to have found himself a candidate with genuine pretensions to giving him that ninth Leger win in Charles St George's Micheletti, a half brother to the owner's good colt Michelozzo, who took the Leger in 1989. Piggott had ridden the unbeaten Micheletti to a silk-smooth victory in York's Melrose Handicap the previous month, after which St George, who died suddenly a few months later, had said: 'One day I'll come back here in a wheelchair and Lester will still be riding.' Although Micheletti was taking a giant stride up in class in the Leger, punters took Lester's phenomenal record in the race into account and latched on to the combination in a big way, forcing him down to 6–1 third favourite. But even Lester's cajoling was not enough and Micheletti had to settle for third place, a long way behind the French-trained winner Toulon.

The Leger might have slipped through his grasp, but against the prosaic backcloth of Town Moor, Lester provided the Doncaster crowds with perhaps the most shimmering display of his talents since he returned almost a year previously. On the second day of the meeting he led off an exquisite family double by driving home a back-to-form Bog Trotter to win the Kiveton Park Stakes for William Haggas. Controlling the pace from the front, Lester mesmerised his rivals, keeping enough in reserve to hold off the furious late thrust of Steve Cauthen on Satin Flower. Having put the American ex-champion in his place, Piggott then proceeded to poleaxe the reigning title holder, Pat Eddery, half an hour later. Riding Mudaffar for Robert Armstrong, Piggott produced the most extraordinary demonstration of tenacity and power to bring the horse from a seemingly impossible position at the rear of the field and shade Eddery's mount, Troupe, by a quivering nostril right on the line.

When Piggott glanced across at Eddery as they sped across the line, his expression seemed to be that of 'a job well done', as Sandy Barclay had once described it. However, it was reported that Lester was cocking a retaliatory snook at Eddery. 'I didn't say anything to him,' Piggott was quoted as saying. 'But as he went past me turning into the straight he had looked at me and laughed.'

'I don't know where they got that story from; it's nonsense,' Eddery says. 'You don't mind getting beaten a short head by Lester. It was marvellous to see him back and riding so well. I think he's as good as ever and he seems much happier and more jokey. It's great to have him back.'

Two days later, in the Reference Point Sceptre Stakes, one of the supporting contests to the Leger, Piggott left another former champion, Willie Carson, reeling with a similar tour de force. Partnering You Know The Rules for Mike Channon, the former England and Southampton footballer turned trainer, Lester again conjured up a last-to-first dash to nose out Carson's mount, Silver Braid.

There were to be other significant successes, notably the victory of Vincent O'Brien's colt, El Prado, who exuded Classic potential when winning at the Curragh, but for professionals and public alike those Doncaster heroics were truly the climax of an unforgettable year of Piggott-watching. And the marvellous thing was that Lester was so obviously revelling in every second of the carnival, too. Friends and colleagues echoed Eddery's remark by saying how much more relaxed Lester seemed as he savoured the feeling of being re-born into the world that was his lifeblood. Joe Mercer's comment was typical. 'He's loving every minute of it. He's into his second childhood,' Mercer said.

Jimmy Lindley was not so sure of Lester's emotional state, however. 'I was chuffed to bits when he won the Breeders' Cup, but really I was sorry to see him come back because I feel concerned for him. He's done enough and I would hate to see him get hurt or go on until he's become a has-been. I think he's in purgatory because he knows he's going to have to quit some time and he's riding on borrowed time.'

As far as the majority were concerned Lester could borrow as much time as he wanted and preferably keep riding until he dropped. Not literally, perhaps; although that is the way he himself would like it, according to Julie Cecil: 'Riding again gave Lester back his raison d'être. He was like a lost soul before he came back. If he fell off and broke his neck that's the way he would like to go.' When Julie adds: 'They broke the mould when they made Lester,' it does not sound such a cliché. Piggott is unique in so many ways and he has brought so much pleasure to millions. Off a horse he is just a man with human shortcomings like the rest of us; it is on horseback that he becomes great and that is what we will always remember.

When Lester finally rides off into the sunset for the last time (but don't bet against another comeback), this tribute from Lindley would make a fitting professional epitaph. 'Lester was racing's genius. He was the best. Nobody will ever follow in his footsteps. The Americans used to say that a cavalry officer would ride a horse until it dropped dead and then an Apache would come along and get it to go another twenty miles. That is how it has been with Lester.'

CHAPTER ELEVEN
THE GOLDEN GUINEAS

Just as we were running out of superlatives, racing's most extraordinary story took another remarkable turn when Piggott, wearing Robert Sangster's green and white silks, steered Rodrigo de Triano to victory in the 2,000 Guineas of 1992, taking his tally of British Classic victories to thirty. The scenes at Newmarket as Piggott brought Rodrigo de Triano back to the winner's enclosure were as emotional as anything we had witnessed during his career. And what made this latest twist in the tale even more incredible was that the second phase of Piggott's career had seemed for a while to be grinding to a halt.

In the six weeks leading up to the Guineas, Piggott had ridden just two winners. With most of the top riders contracted to leading owners, Piggott was finding quality mounts difficult to come by and he was often having to scratch around for rides and winding up on the back of moderate horses trained by minor-league trainers.

Lester had tried to get back in with Sangster on a regular basis the previous year, but the millionaire owner had rejected his advances. At the beginning of 1991, Sangster had installed Peter Chapple-Hyam at the helm of Manton, his multi-million pound training complex in Wiltshire. Chapple-Hyam was in his first season as a licensed trainer, having been assistant to the previous Manton incumbent, Barry Hills, and had made a superb start to his career. Sangster says: 'Lester came up to me at the Sales and said that he would like to be first jockey at Manton and I said "Sorry, Lester, but we've been through all this before". I might have considered it if I'd had an older man in charge of Manton, but it wouldn't have been fair to a young trainer like Peter if Lester had started getting up to his old tricks. He had messed Barry Hills around at Doncaster when he got off one of his horses to ride In The Groove at Goodwood and Barry said to me "Nothing's changed with Lester".'

Whatever his view of Piggott's reliability, Sangster had certainly not lost faith in his ability in the saddle. Willie Carson had ridden Rodrigo de Triano to the two major victories of his unbeaten juvenile career, the Champagne Stakes at Doncaster and the Middle Park Stakes at Newmarket, but when Carson was

163

claimed by Hamdan Al Maktoum to ride Muhtarram in the Guineas the Sangster team moved in unhesitatingly for Piggott.

Ironically, it was Chapple-Hyam who suggested Piggott as Carson's replacement and Sangster readily concurred. 'When we knew Carson would not be available we considered Cash Asmussen and Lanfranco Dettori [the young Italian who had turned down the offer of a retainer from Sangster shortly before the Guineas], but we had noticed that Rodrigo had developed a tendency to pull up when he got in front on the gallops, so we decided that Lester was the ideal man to settle him and bring him on the scene as late as possible,' Sangster explains.

Chapple-Hyam recalls his phone call to Piggott with some amusement. 'When I rang Lester up before the Guineas and offered him the ride he just grunted and said "Okay". I asked him to come up to Manton and gallop the horse in the morning and he said to me "What time do you pull out from the yard?" When I told him 7.30 a.m. he mumbled "That's a bit early for me these days". Nevertheless, he turned up right on time. He never says much, but after he had galloped Rodrigo you could tell he was a bit excited.'

Named after the man who spotted land from the crow's nest on Christopher Columbus's ship the *Santa María*, Rodrigo de Triano was a son of El Gran Senor, who was Sangster's last British Classic winner when he took the 2,000 Guineas in 1984. Rodrigo de Triano had been the star among a wealth of prodigious talent in Chapple-Hyam's yard in 1991 and went into retirement in the winter as clear favourite for the Guineas. However, his reputation suffered a knock when he was beaten into fourth place on his first appearance as a three-year-old behind the French-trained Lion Cavern in the Greenham Stakes at Newbury.

Bookmakers pushed Rodrigo de Triano's odds out several points for the Guineas, but Chapple-Hyam and Sangster were unconcerned. Chapple-Hyam admitted publicly that the colt had been some way short of peak fitness at Newbury and he also pointed out that the soft ground had been against his horse. There was still an unwavering faith in Rodrigo de Triano's ability to win the Newmarket Classic and Sangster, who had backed him at 10–1 during the winter, was tempted to wade in again when he saw 6–1 being offered at Newmarket on the day of the race.

Others remained unconvinced, however. There had been a scare the week before the Guineas when Rodrigo de Triano injured a heel, but that had not been too serious a problem and some of the doubters were not so much questioning the horse's ability as the jockey's. On the morning of the Guineas, John McCririck and John Francome, two of the resident experts on Channel Four's weekly racing programme, *The Morning Line*, made it clear that as far as an important race like the Guineas was concerned they believed Piggott was quite simply past it. McCririck was particularly scathing, suggesting that it was a mistake to give Piggott the ride and that there would be grounds for recrimination if the fifty-six-year-old grandfather was beaten in a photo-finish.

As Piggott took Rodrigo de Triano to post in that familiar pose, bottom perched high above the saddle, his face as ever an inscrutable mask, the punters clearly had their doubts, too. Rodrigo de Triano was easy to back in the market, drifting out from 5–1 to 6–1 as money poured on the Arab-owned Alnasr Alwasheek, the fluent winner of Newmarket's Craven Stakes, forcing him down to 5–2 favourite.

As the sixteen runners burst from the stalls, it could be seen quite clearly that Rodrigo de Triano had got away last of all. In retrospect it is clear that this was a typically audacious ploy by Lester to enable him to get his mount settled before he made any serious attempt to take a hand at the business end of the race. Piggott was happy to lob along at the rear until almost halfway, but when he made his move it became instantly clear how ominously well he was travelling. If Michael Roberts had taken a look back as he drove the fancied Pursuit Of Love into the lead with some three furlongs to run he would have seen a sight to send a shiver down his spine.

Bringing Rodrigo de Triano through the pack with the sort of untroubled run that only he can educe with such certainty, Lester surged up to Pursuit Of Love and sent his mount scuttling past into a clear lead as the cheering began to rock the stands. The outsider Lucky Lindy came with a strong, late burst that carried him past Pursuit Of Love into second place, but Lester was already easing off the throttle. The hallmark of Piggott's riding has so often been his ability to make it all look so simple and if any other jockey had been aboard Rodrigo de Triano you have to wonder whether the prize would have been plundered with such elegance and economy of effort.

So the celebrations began. Newmarket is frequently a cold and soulless place to be, but as Lester eased his way back through the frenzied crowds the warmth of the welcome made the afternoon seem like glorious summer as those fortunate enough to be there savoured a moment that would linger in the memory for years.

Lester's reponse was a series of uninhibited smiles that lit up that furrowed face in an expression of sheer delight. By his standards he was positively effusive as the media homed in on him. 'I've always maintained my fitness and I was lucky to be on the right horse,' he said. 'They went faster than I thought they would early on, but Rodrigo was always going so easily that he would have won even if he hadn't stayed the distance.'

Some still seemed to have difficulty in believing that Piggott had brought it off, notably Brough Scott, whose preoccupation with Lester's age in the post-race interview for Channel Four elicited a nice line in repartee. 'So there you are, a fifty-six-year-old grandfather, Lester. Did you really think this could happen?' Scott asked. 'Why not?' Lester replied with a shrug of the shoulders, looking surprised that the question had been asked. Pursuing his theme, Scott followed up by asking 'But how much longer can you really go on, Lester?' The response came back quick as a flash. 'I've got one in the fifth race,' Lester said with a grin.

As the revelry continued in the unsaddling enclosure Chapple-Hyam and Sangster paid their tributes. 'I was never worried about putting Lester up. He was riding winners before I was born and he's still as good as ever, probably better,' Chapple-Hyam said. 'People say he never follows orders, but he followed mine to the letter. I told him to track Pursuit Of Love and he did just that. When I told him not to go to the front too soon or Rodrigo might pull up he told me "They won't even see me coming".'

Sangster, clearly elated at ending his Classic drought, said: 'When I saw the odds they were offering on Rodrigo de Triano before the race I thought they were terrific value and I was tempted to back him again, but I didn't want to be greedy. The betting wasn't what was important. I was just delighted for Peter, who is the youngest trainer, and for Lester, who is the oldest jockey.

'I think Lester is the greatest jockey of this century and of the previous century as well. The crowd love him and that's what racing's all about. It's an entertainment business and Lester's the best in the business.'

At moments like those it is easy to go over the top, but it is surely fair to say that Piggott's thirtieth Classic triumph in his fifty-seventh year must rank as one of the great moments of sport. 'He's Just Incredible!' the headline in the *Racing Post* read the following Monday. That summed it up perfectly.

CHAPTER TWELVE
MR INDESTRUCTIBLE

Besides his enduring magic in the saddle, one thing Lester Piggott has never lost throughout his unparalleled career is the ability to play fast and loose with our emotions. And the sight of that painfully spare frame sprawled in the dirt in the white-hot glare of Florida's Gulfstream Park following a horrific fall in the 1992 Breeders' Cup made us all sick to the stomach.

In those heart-stopping moments when Piggott's mount, Mr Brooks, crumpled to the ground with a shattered leg in the opening event of the $10 million programme, pinning Piggott beneath his stricken carcass like a rag doll, it looked as if we were witnessing not merely a tragic end to his career but something far worse.

Piggott lay pale and ominously still while quick-thinking spectators dragged Mr Brooks off him and the paramedics sped into action. Within seconds the phone lines in the press room were crackling as reporters frantically fed back the news of the accident together with the horrendous early prognostications. From the grandstand one could only guess at the extent of Piggott's injuries, but the early feedback was bad and many of us genuinely feared for his life or assumed that he would at the very least be permanently crippled.

We had reckoned without one all-important factor, however – Piggott's superhuman capacity for survival. He was to shrug off that Florida fall and bounce back into action as if he had merely suffered a bad bout of flu. Combine that episode with the thought that he had come within a hair's breadth of death in a traumatic plane journey three months earlier and you began to feel that even a nuclear explosion might not knock this bionic grandfather out of his stride.

For a short while at least, though, we could be forgiven for having our doubts. As Piggott was loaded into the ambulance at Gulfstream, he had been given an oxygen mask to help him breathe and was also wearing a neck brace. What was visible of his haggard face was contorted in pain and smeared with blood. It was initially feared that the crushing impact of Mr Brooks landing on top of him might have left him with many broken bones, including his spine, and also caused massive internal injuries.

Heads I win: Lester comes with another of those irresistible finishes on Mr Brooks to edge out Pat Eddery on Pursuit Of Love and Walter Swinburn on Sheikh Albadou in Newmarket's July Cup.

The fall of Mr Brooks was as bizarre as it was sickening and in retrospect it is clear that Lester not only suspected what was about to happen well before it actually did, but also orchestrated the final moments of the drama to avoid injury to a fellow rider and with almost complete disregard for his own safety.

Mr Brooks had earned the right to challenge America's leading sprinters with victories in the Prix de l'Abbaye at Longchamp and the July Cup at Newmarket, where Piggott produced another of those mesmerising finishes to inch out Pat Eddery on Pursuit Of Love and Walter Swinburn on Sheikh Albadou, winner of the previous year's Breeders' Cup Sprint in Kentucky.

The stifling humidity of Florida in late October was to wipe out the seemingly powerful British challenge for the seven-race series at Gulfstream as effectively as if the horses had been administered a stopping drug. Piggott's dual 2,000 Guineas winner, Rodrigo de Triano, was seriously fancied to add another memorable chapter to the great comeback story by winning the $3 million Classic at the end of the day, but Swinburn, deputising for the injured Piggott, found himself aboard a horse that was a shadow of the European champion he had proved himself to be as he trailed home last of all behind A. P. Indy.

But, with the memory of the previous year's successes at Churchill Downs to buoy them, the visitors' hopes were sky high as Sheikh Albadou and Mr Brooks were led to the start on Gulfstream's palm-fringed circuit. Sheikh Albadou was thought to be Britain's chief hope for the $1 million Sprint, which he had won in such style at Churchill Downs twelve months earlier, but there was a good deal of quiet confidence behind Mr Brooks, who represented the prolific stable of Richard Hannon, crowned champion trainer for the first time in 1992.

Even before they entered the stalls, though, Piggott began to feel uneasy. He was reported to have said to Swinburn on Sheikh Albadou that he felt Mr Brooks was moving badly and this led to implicit criticism of Piggott on American television, with an NBC commentator suggesting that Piggott should have taken the opportunity to withdraw Mr Brooks.

Once the runners had been despatched, Piggott lay towards the rear of the fourteen-horse field and had made only minimal progress when the drama occurred. The fall itself seemed almost to happen in slow motion, like a scene from some badly made B-movie, with Mr Brooks crumpling gradually before ending in a heap on top of Piggott.

Piggott said later: 'I remember Mr Brooks going down, but I don't recall anything after that until I woke up in the ambulance. I knew something was wrong as soon as we started to make the turn and I knew Mr Brooks was going to go twenty yards before it happened.'

Piggott expanded further on the accident in an interview with his daughter, Tracy. 'I looked round when I felt him go. I knew there was another horse behind me. The jockey shouted. He was on my inside. There was no room and I did not want him to go on top of me, so I held Mr Brooks up after his leg broke for as long as I could to make sure there was enough room for the other horse to get through.'

Piggott went on: 'Most times when horses break a leg they don't go down, but his just broke off. When I hit the ground I thought I had taken an easy fall. But then Mr Brooks caught up with me and instead of rolling away he rolled into me.'

Mr Brooks was destroyed by lethal injection, and one of the first things Piggott was to say when he sat up in hospital just a few hours later, apart from asking what won the race, was to express his sadness over the loss of such a good and brave horse. He watched the fall over and over on the news as he sat up in bed in intensive care in Florida's Hollywood Memorial Hospital tucking into a bowl of jelly.

Piggott and his jelly certainly caught the imagination. A headline in the *Racing Post* read 'Jelly-eating Pushes Bush off the Front', highlighting the fact that even

Before the fall: Piggott on Mr Brooks on his way to the start for the Breeders' Cup Sprint at Gulfstream Park. Minutes later he was lying battered and bloodied in the dirt after his mount's fatal accident.

President Bush's fight for survival in the American elections had been upstaged by Piggott's accident. The *Post*'s analysis of the newspaper coverage given to Piggott in the British press mentioned the *Daily Telegraph*'s line that 'Bush was wobbling, so too was Major, and Piggott . . . he was eating jelly'.

The injuries Piggott sustained were, in the circumstances, relatively light. He broke a collar bone and two ribs and had a badly gashed head. He also suffered a partially collapsed lung, which gave rise to some anxiety for a while. It had been feared that he had damaged his spleen, but that was discounted by medical staff. He underwent a brain scan, but that was only precautionary.

The morning after the accident he apparently did not even have a headache and was in remarkably good spirits. The only thing he complained about was the vast amount of sand coming out of his nose and ears which made his bed resemble a

This dramatic video image captures the awful moment when Mr Brooks, having shattered a leg, begins to crumple to the ground.

stretch of the nearby Hollywood beach. The speed of his recovery amazed the doctors, one of whom told Tracy that he had never seen a man of Piggott's age anywhere near as fit and wanted to use him as a medical exhibit!

Lester was out of hospital in time for his fifty-seventh birthday five days after the accident and then spent a week recuperating in the Florida sunshine. A picture on the front page of the *Sporting Life* showing him enjoying champagne and a huge cigar in the company of Tracy, with the only visible legacy of the accident a bruise under his left eye, gladdened many a heart back home in Britain.

As Piggott's adoring public breathed a collective sigh of relief at the news that the old warrior was very much alive and kicking, there was a concerned communication from a long-standing patron that seemed to bear a special significance. The Queen faxed a personal get-well message which was delivered to

What's all the fuss about? Lester, seen here enjoying a cigar, a glass of champagne and the attention of his daughter Tracy, was quick to shrug off the effects of his horrific accident as he recuperated in the Florida sunshine.

Piggott in hospital by the British Consul. It read: 'I am terribly sorry to hear about your accident and hope you make a quick recovery.' Two months earlier Piggott had pulled on the Royal livery to provide the Queen with a major success in Germany when he drove Sharp Prod home to win the Group Two Moet & Chandon-Rennen at Baden-Baden.

Those few words of sympathy from Her Majesty plus the fact that he had ridden winners for the Queen and her racing manager, Lord Carnarvon, in the preceding weeks, added further fuel to suggestions that Piggott would soon be given back his OBE, which he had forfeited four years earlier during his time in prison. It was also felt that he might even be awarded the knighthood that his achievements had long merited but which had almost certainly been prevented by his incarceration.

Speaking in May 1993, just before this book went to press, a spokesman for the Honours Department at 10 Downing Street seemed to suggest that the way was in fact open for Piggott to receive one or both honours. The spokesman said that there was no set rule when it comes to awarding honours and each case is looked at on its individual merits. He added that Piggott's term in gaol could not be seen as an insurmountable barrier to such an award.

For those few days that Piggott lay in hospital, however, it was not so much the possibility of 'Arise, Sir Lester' that dominated the headlines as the question of whether he would ever ride again. Even though it was soon established that his injuries were not in themselves sufficient to prevent him getting back into the saddle, there were calls from many so-called well-wishers urging him to quit while he was still in one piece. Most of those retirement notices came from sports writers who seemed to feel it was their paternalistic duty to call time on the great man. Those self-appointed Piggott guardians totally failed to allow for the fact that race riding was almost as precious to Piggott as life itself.

As far as racing professionals were concerned there was virtually unanimous feeling that Lester could and should ride again. Robert Sangster's remarks were typical: 'Carry on, Lester – that's what I say. I think he should carry on riding as long as he wants to. He can keep on riding for me for as long as he likes.'

John Gosden, the Newmarket trainer, commented: 'They never made any rules about Lester and we'd better not start now. He is his own man and does his own thing and I'm sure that's how it will continue.'

Geoff Wragg, one of Gosden's colleagues, said: 'Who are we to tell Lester what to do? People doubted him when he made his comeback, but look what he's done since then, winning all those Group One races. No one can tell LP when to finish.'

That anyone should even think of doing so totally amazed Lester. 'Of course I will ride again. What else would I do?' Lester said. 'If it had happened at Chepstow there wouldn't have been all this bother. I've had worse falls tumbling out of bed.

'I'm lucky because I can put up with a lot of things and one of them is pain,' he told the *Sporting Life*. 'Nothing bothers me. They're going to stuff me when I go! If you like to do something enough it overcomes all other thoughts. The pain doesn't last long. I ride because I love to do it. Racing is dangerous but so are a lot of things. I'd rather die in bed than on a racetrack covered in dirt, but we all have to go some time. You are born to do something and you might as well do it.'

Piggott added that he could ride again in three weeks if he wanted to and ride out within a fortnight. In the end he realised that it might be prudent to allow even his bionic body a little more time to recover and he eventually climbed back into the saddle competitively three months later in Dubai.

Piggott also said that he had been far more frightened by the near miss he had been involved in during a plane flight to York races in August. Just how near to oblivion he had come was revealed in the official report on the incident which came out in March 1993. The report stated that Piggott and three fellow jockeys, Michael Hills, Philip Robinson and George Duffield, had come within ten feet of death when an RAF Tornado, on a routine exercise from RAF Coningsby in Lincolnshire, roared past their light aircraft.

Piggott and his colleagues were twenty minutes into their journey from Newmarket to York's Ebor meeting when four RAF Tornadoes catapulted past the jockeys' plane, a twin-engined Piper Seneca PA34. The Piper was flipped over by a jet slipstream.

Piggott said: 'It was very frightening. It nearly blew us away and we all finished up in the roof of the plane. The jet came up from nowhere and it left a space devoid of air and we just dropped into it.'

Robinson gave his version of the nightmare by saying: 'I was in the front with the pilot, David Smith. The RAF aircraft suddenly came up very fast and shot past feet away. It was so close that our pilot and I thought we had been hit. I thought we'd all be dead. It was as close as you can come to being killed and still survive. The pilot hit his head on the roof and several of us had cricked necks as well. Then our plane dropped 200 feet. I was frightened to death.'

Hills said: 'I was fast asleep and Lester was reading the paper. We were about 4,500 feet up when we were suddenly surrounded by these planes. One passed so close we thought it would hit us. Our plane turned a somersault and Lester ended up on top of George mumbling, "What's happening?" '

Duffield went on to win the Yorkshire Oaks on User Friendly later that afternoon with his ribs strapped up after being bruised in the incident and he said: 'I was asleep. I woke up and found Lester's head in my lap.'

The plane made an emergency landing at an RAF base near Doncaster and after inspecting for damage Smith decided it was safe to carry on. 'It wasn't a near miss, it was a very near miss,' he said.

In the official report which was published seven months later, the Joint Airmiss Working Group (JAWG) revealed that the fighter pilot appeared to see the Piper a split second before the potential collision and rolled the jet over so its belly skimmed past. It put the incident, which took place over Lincolnshire, into the rare A category of air misses in which there is a real risk of collision and said that the Tornado would have hit the Piper if the pilot had not rolled left, passing 'no more than ten feet' in front of the Piper.

The crowds who poured into York on Ebor day, the centrepiece of the three-day August meeting which is often referred to as the Royal Ascot of the North, were blissfully ignorant of the fact that they might so easily have been mourning

Piggott instead of acclaiming his genius once again.

The Knavesmire was still buzzing from another supreme piece of Piggott artistry the previous afternoon when his riding of Rodrigo de Triano in the Juddmonte International Stakes elicited the headlines 'Peerless Piggott' in the *Sporting Life* and 'Rodrigo Showstopper' in the *Racing Post*. In his front-page report in the *Life*, Geoff Lester wrote: 'There are jockeys – and then there is Lester Piggott! The 56-year-old Long Fellow rolled back the years to land an emotional success on Rodrigo de Triano in the Juddmonte International Stakes at York yesterday. On the forty-fourth anniversary of riding his first winner on The Chase at Haydock when only a twelve-year-old, the legendary granddad gained his fifth success in the race following Dahlia (twice), Hawaiian Sound and Commanche Run.'

Lester went on: 'In as hot a Group One race as there has been all season, surely nobody except the remarkable Piggott would have had the audacity to give his classy opponents so much start . . . this was Lester at his best and as the maestro steered Rodrigo into the winner's enclosure the crescendo of noise built up like a last night at the Proms.'

After Piggott had brought Rodrigo through from last to first in the straight to out down the Oaks runner-up, All At Sea, Peter Chapple-Hyam, Rodrigo's trainer, described the occasion as 'the greatest day of my life apart from the day I got married'. Chapple-Hyam recalls: 'I went to shake Lester's hand afterwards and he put his arms round me. I've never seen Lester so excited.'

Rodrigo's owner-breeder, Robert Sangster, said that he had won a total of 105 Group races but that none had given him more pleasure than this one. 'Having bred Rodrigo makes the win extra special. It hurt when people said we were wrong to run him in the Derby. I still feel we were right to go to Epsom, but Rodrigo did not come down the hill.

'The first person I saw when I arrived at York was Lester and I thought he was going to tap me for the fare!' Sangster joked. 'He came over and asked me how he should ride Rodrigo from the outside draw. He reminded me that he had got some stick for dropping out Rodrigo at Epsom, but I told him to ride the same race. It's the first time he has ever asked me for advice – maybe I'll become his consultant!'

Sangster's levity was not so well received by everyone. His reference to the Derby highlighted an unfortunate low spot in the partnership of Lester and Rodrigo which had woven a golden thread through the 1992 Flat season.

Following Rodrigo's 2,000 Guineas triumph, Piggott had ridden him to an equally smooth success in the Irish equivalent at the Curragh where he demonstrated the kind of sixth sense that allows him to anticipate what is going to happen in a race long before it does. There were only six runners in the Irish Classic, including the English 2,000 Guineas runner-up, Lucky Lindy, and Piggott waited at the tail-end of the field until approaching the final furlong where the other five formed a seemingly impenetrable barrier in front of him. Piggott was quite clearly going best and we were entitled to assume that he would pull round his rivals and challenge on the wide outside. Suddenly, though, he made a lunge towards the rail where there appeared to be only a solid wall of horseflesh. For a moment it seemed as if he had suffered a rare brainstorm, but we should have known better. A gap suddenly opened up like the Red Sea and Piggott was through it and away. It was breathtaking stuff and only he could have carried it off.

Then came the great debate as to whether Rodrigo should run in the Derby. Sangster knew that, on breeding, Rodrigo's chance of lasting the mile and a half was doubtful to say the least. A son of his outstanding 2,000 Guineas winner, El Gran Senor, who had been outstayed by Secreto in the 1984 Derby, Rodrigo de Triano was out of Hot Princess, who was a miler. Sangster agonised for some while before committing Rodrigo to Epsom, but the decision seemed more in the 'why not have a go?' spirit rather than any serious conviction that he would win.

Most pundits dismissed Rodrigo's chances, but the possibility of Piggott riding to a fabulous tenth Derby success captured the public imagination and Rodrigo de Triano started 13–2 favourite at Epsom. He was never in with a chance and finished ninth of the eighteen runners behind Chapple-Hyam's other runner, Dr Devious, the second favourite, who gave his young trainer a remarkable third Classic success in his second season.

Rodrigo's flop was followed by some ridiculous allegations as certain ill-informed members of the media and the public sought to make something more sinister out of Piggott's 'easy ride' on the horse. Yes, Piggott had been easy on Rodrigo, but for a very good reason, as Chapple-Hyam explains: 'Rodrigo didn't stay the Derby distance, but besides that a lot of my horses were sick before Epsom. We isolated Rodrigo and Dr Devious, but Rodrigo coughed quite a few times after the Derby. Lester sensed he wasn't right during the race and that was why he wasn't too hard on him. Anyone else but Lester would have given him a hard race and ruined him for the rest of the season.'

Rodrigo reappeared at Royal Ascot a fortnight later and Piggott was again criticised for giving the horse too much to do after he finished fourth behind Brief Truce. He was beaten by less than two lengths, though, and finished in front of the so-called French wonder colt, Arazi, who started a red-hot favourite.

Chapple-Hyam takes up the story again. 'Rodrigo was still not right at Royal Ascot. All my horses ran badly there and we virtually shut up shop for six weeks after the meeting. Dr Devious came back with a temperature of 105° after he was beaten by St Jovite in the Irish Derby a fortnight after Ascot.'

This effectively answers those who suggested there should have been a stewards' inquiry into Rodrigo's improvement when he came back to win the Juddmonte International at York, where he proved that he stayed a mile and a quarter if not a mile and a half. There was to be another superb victory over that

'Oh, no – it's bloody Lester again!' Willie Carson on Lahib can hardly believe his eyes as Piggott swoops in the last seventy-five yards to win the Champion Stakes at Newmarket aboard Rodrigo de Triano.

distance in the Champion Stakes at Newmarket in October, when Piggott produced Rodrigo so late that the usually effervescent Willie Carson on the runner-up, Lahib, was left shaking his head in disbelief after being collared in the last seventy-five yards.

'I thought I had it won, but then I saw Rodrigo out of the corner of my eye and thought, "Oh, no, it's bloody Lester!" ' Carson said. Explaining that Rodrigo's participation had been in doubt until the last minute because of two injury scares during the previous week, Chapple-Hyam said: 'Lester told me that I had left him short of work after he returned today and told me not to do it again!'

No amount of work could have prepared Rodrigo for the oppressive heat of Florida. Allied to the fact that he hated the dirt being kicked in his face and the dreadful circumstances of Piggott's earlier injury, it produced a sad end to Rodrigo's racing career as he trailed home unhappily in the Breeders' Cup Classic.

Rodrigo de Triano aside, there had been other memorable moments for Piggott during the 1992 season, although his tally of thirty-five domestic winners from 329 rides was surprisingly low. That could be attributed partly to the new-style riding contracts mentioned in a previous chapter whereby jockeys signed for owners rather than trainers. Piggott found it increasingly difficult to pick and choose the best horses at will as he had done in the first phase of his career, even though he was still widely regarded as being peerless on the big occasion, as demonstrated by the fact that he amassed more than £1.1 million in prize money at home and abroad and rode eight Group One winners.

There was another Royal Ascot success to thrill punters and champagne quaffers alike when Lester rode Niche, who was owned by the Queen's racing manager, Lord Carnarvon, to a hard-fought victory over the hot favourite, Silver Wizard, in the Norfolk Stakes. Lester struck up a memorable partnership with Niche, guiding her to an easy win in the Lowther Stakes at York in August and going on to even greater achievements the following year.

Simply the best: Having nearly come down twice early on, Lester, whip raised, drives Thamestar ahead in the final strides at Doncaster in a finish that Channel Four viewers voted their favourite Piggott performance of the 1992 season.

Reappearing in the Nell Gwyn Stakes in the spring of 1993, Niche was expected to play only a supporting role against potential Classic fillies like Sayyedati and Bashayer, but Piggott nipped off in front and was never headed, coming home clear of Zarani Sidi Anna, with the hot favourite, Sayyedati, only third. Niche and Piggott were again considered only bit-part players in the 1,000 Guineas, but they almost stole the show, leading until a furlong from home when Walter Swinburn drove Sayyedati past. Niche rallied well under Lester's urgings and there was only half a length in it at the line.

Of all the successes he gained in 1992, though, it was his victory on Thamestar in a relatively minor affair at Doncaster that arguably stood out as the most compelling piece of vintage Piggott theatre. Viewers of Channel Four certainly thought so because they voted Thamestar's win their number one choice from ten of Lester's best wins that season in a poll on *The Morning Line*.

Thamestar's victory was Lester's last before the horrors of Gulfstream and those watching him through their binoculars in the early stages of the Doncaster event might have thought for one fleeting moment that they were about to witness yet another disaster in Piggott's accident-prone career. The incident happened not long after the start of the North America Travel Service Handicap when Thamestar twice fly-jumped, throwing Piggott up on his neck. Piggott was in real danger of ending up on the floor and, as he was lying in fifth place on the inside in a tightly bunched field, he would have become a human football in a pack of flying hooves had he gone down. As it was he had to rein Thamestar back and although he managed to prevent his mount from taking a tumble the seriousness of the incident can be gauged by the fact that Piggott asked the Channel Four team if they would show the film twice.

Lester explained those perilous few moments by saying: 'Thamestar went over one hill and then thought there was another coming up, took off again and took a long time to come down!'

After that it might have been expected that Thamestar's chance would have disappeared, not just because he forfeited so much ground and dropped right back to the rear, but also because any other rider might have been so fazed by the incident that he would have been happy to come home in one piece, never mind think about getting back into the race. But, Lester being Lester, the drama was treated merely as a minor blip. Threading his way through the seventeen-strong field he began to close relentlessly on the leaders in the straight. Fifty yards from the finish his task still looked impossible as Simonov and First Bid duelled nose to nose for the line. Then Lester got down to ride one of those superhuman finishes reminiscent of The Minstrel in the Derby or Royal Academy in the Breeders' Cup. Whip flailing, he jolted Thamestar forward as if with the aid of some unseen force propelling the horse from behind. Twenty yards from the line he was still going to be third at best; at the post he had thrust Thamestar's head in front of Simonov's for the most extraordinary win in a four-horse photo. Piggott's unfortunate victim was once again Pat Eddery, who went on to take the Racing Post Trophy half an hour later on Armiger. One can only guess at Eddery's thoughts after Piggott had stolen the prize from under his nose, but they were probably unprintable.

Channel Four viewers also voted Piggott the Racing Personality of the Year in another poll which demonstrated his popularity in the most remarkable way. Despite the competition of such notable contemporaries as the crowd-pleasing South African, Michael Roberts, who ended Eddery's reign as champion jockey in 1992, the supreme National Hunt champion, Peter Scudamore, and twelve other rivals, Piggott polled an amazing 60 per cent of the vote.

A guest appearance on *The Morning Line* the following season confirmed how much Lester had changed in personal terms since his return to race riding, continuing to come across as far more relaxed and outgoing than the Piggott of old. Beaming throughout and responding willingly to his questioners, Piggott delighted the viewers with some nifty one-liners. For example, when asked what he did when trainers tried to give him orders, he replied with tongue firmly in cheek, 'Well, you've got to listen . . .!'

Piggott received two more accolades in the next few months, the first being the Personality of the Year at the prestigious Cartier Awards less than three weeks after his fall at Gulfstream. Piggott received a hero's welcome when he appeared at the glittering black-tie affair looking remarkably fit and composed and he proceeded to surprise the delighted audience with an uncharacteristically voluble speech.

For the third year running, Piggott also picked up the Personality of the Year award from the Jockeys' Association. When he went up to receive his latest trophy at the dinner in London to the accompaniment of 'Simply the Best', his colleagues once again showed their affection and respect for him in the most vociferous way.

After his Breeders' Cup accident, Lester returned to race riding in Dubai in early February 1993, booting home two winners at the Jebel Ali racecourse on the second day of his comeback. Piggott showed his pleasure by saying: 'Not bad was it? It has been a long time and I have missed riding. By the law of averages a fall like that has to happen some time. Sometimes you just have to take a risk if you want to win.'

Piggott went on to Hong Kong, landing his first winners there for seven years. He also sustained yet another injury, requiring stitches for a cut above his eye when one of his mounts flung its head back and banged him in the face.

So it was back to Britain again and as the 1993 Flat season began to take shape Lester was showing no sign of any legacy from his fall, nor indeed was there any indication that anno Domini might finally be gaining ground on him. He never really looked like gaining another 2,000 Guineas success, fading into fifth place on Silver Wizard behind the brilliant Zafonic after cutting out the early pace, but he

Still out in front: Piggott's judgement showed no sign of faltering in his fifty-eighth year. Here he times it to perfection on Swing Low in the 1993 Lockinge Stakes at Newbury.

went close in the 1,000 Guineas on Niche and even closer on Vincent O'Brien's Fatherland, who was beaten a head by Barathea in the Irish 2,000 Guineas, and overall the magic shone out as brightly as it ever had.

There was a particularly golden day for the fans at Kempton Park on the May Bank Holiday when Lester booted home a long-priced treble, his first three-timer since he made that phoenix-like rise from retirement. His riding of Brockton Dancer at Kempton provided a little gem of tactical brilliance. Employing what might best be described as legitimate gamesmanship, Lester kept Ray Cochrane on the favourite, Toocando, shut in on his inside for long enough to make Cochrane's eventual switch to the outside just too late to succeed.

In one sense such Piggott masterpieces provoked mixed emotions. We knew that even he could not cheat time forever and, no matter how much longer he carried on, those works of art were inevitably limited editions. With that thought at the back of the mind each victory was savoured that much more.

The basis of our deep-seated affection for the man who has engendered such a wide range of emotions throughout his extraordinary career was summed up eloquently by Christopher Poole in the *Evening Standard* in a fulsome personal tribute to Lester written shortly after the Gulfstream fall.

Poole began: 'Lester Piggott, that most durable of British sporting institutions, has survived another crisis. At a time of life when walking the dog comprises a major physical effort for normal mortals, this fabled jockey dismisses any thought of retirement following his horrific mid-race fall in Florida. And the collective sigh of relief that his injuries are not, after all, what the Americans call career threatening, is audible throughout this country and far beyond . . .'

Poole went on: 'So why is this curious man, a convicted tax-dodger who speaks in monosyllables and never seeks public adulation, so loved and admired? . . . Piggott does not fit the hero stereotype. His deeply creased face and grey hair; his congenital deafness and a body emaciated by years of self-denial combine to make him any casting director's nightmare . . . An abiding love of money is perceived as a character weakness. It certainly led to his conviction and imprisonment for attempting to defraud the tax authorities.

'Yet, this ageing, solitary figure is able to produce a natural charm which captivates all who meet him. When he rewards you with that rare, lopsided smile and a word or two, the temptation is to walk up to perfect strangers and boast that you know the Turf superstar and have just spoken to him.

'That Lester Piggott has been an acquaintance of mine for more than thirty years is a source of pride, silly as that might sound. But the fact of the matter is that only a handful of people can claim intimate friendship with the world's greatest jockey, so to be rated worth a token "good morning" or even a nod of recognition carries status.'

Poole concluded: 'But it is, of course, his oneness with the thoroughbred horse which makes Piggott unique. The thrill of watching that paper-thin body, posed in an eternal question mark, as he drives for the winning post is unmatched throughout sport.'

And so say all of us.

CHRONOLOGY OF
LESTER PIGGOTT'S CAREER

1948: At the age of twelve becomes officially apprenticed to father, Keith, at their Lambourn stables. First public ride on The Chase at Salisbury on 7 April. First winner on The Chase at Haydock Park on 18 August, his only success of the season.

1949: Gains second success after gap of a year and rides only six winners from 120 mounts that season.

1950: Rides fifty-two winners and takes title of champion apprentice. First ride at Royal Ascot on Eastern Saga, unplaced in Ascot Stakes.

1951: Retains apprentice title with fifty-one victories, despite breaking leg and missing last quarter of season. Gains first major success on French-trained Mystery IX in Eclipse Stakes and first of 114 victories at Royal Ascot on Malka's Boy in Wokingham Stakes. Finishes unplaced on first Derby mount, Zucchero, after being left at start.

1952: Finishes second in Derby on Gay Time, beaten by Charlie Smirke on Tulyar. Rides seventy-nine winners and finishes fifth in jockeys' table.

1953: Wins Coronation Cup at Epsom on Zucchero, but manages only forty-one winners as his weight increases. During the winter he successfully tries his hand at jumping, gaining nine wins from twenty-five rides.

1954: Gains first of nine Derby wins on Never Say Die at 33–1 at the age of eighteen, but has only forty-one other winners that year. Receives six-month suspension for his riding of Never Say Die in King Edward VII Stakes at Royal Ascot two weeks later, after being found guilty of interfering with Sir Gordon Richards on Rashleigh. Made to leave his father and work for Jack Jarvis in Newmarket. During his suspension Richards retires. Ban lifted at end of September.

1955: Becomes first jockey to Noel Murless at Warren Place.

Finishes third in jockeys' table with 103 winners.

1956: Third in championship again with 129 victories.

1957: Wins first 2,000 Guineas and second Derby on Crepello, first Oaks on Carrozza, first Ascot Gold Cup on Zarathustra and first German Derby on Orsini. Third in table with 122 successes.

1958: Wins Ascot Gold Cup on Gladness, first ride for Vincent O'Brien. Sixth in championship with eighty-three wins.

1959: Wins Oaks, Sussex Stakes, Yorkshire Oaks and Champion Stakes on Petite Etoile. Third in championship with 142 wins.

1960: Wins Derby and first of eight St Legers on St Paddy. Takes first of eleven jockeys' titles with a total of 170 successes. Marries Susan Armstrong on 22 February.

1961: Rides 164 winners to finish second in championship to Scobie Breasley. No ride in Derby after his intended mount, Pinturischio, is doped. Wins St Leger on Aurelius.

1962: Suspended for two months for allegedly not trying hard enough on Ione at Lincoln. Fourth in table with ninety-six wins.

1963: Second in table with 175 wins. Father, Keith, trains Ayala to win the Grand National at 66–1.

1964: Takes second jockeys' title (beginning a run of eight straight wins) with 140 victories despite bad fall from Persian Garden at Longchamp in September which keeps him out for three weeks. Gains first French Classic win on Rajput Princess in French 1,000 Guineas.

1965: Third title with 160 wins. Gains first Irish Classic success on Meadow Court in Irish Derby. Also first of seven wins in King George VI and Queen Elizabeth Stakes on Meadow Court. Rides eight winners at Royal Ascot. Only Sir Gordon Richards with nine has bettered this total.

1966: Wins Oaks on Valoris for Vincent O'Brien after choosing her in preference to Varinia trained by Noel Murless. This precipitates split between Murless and Piggott. Records highest ever total of 191 wins for fourth championship, with the highest ever winning margin (ninety-four over Scobie Breasley).

1967: Rides as freelance for the first time. Finishes second on Ribocco in Derby, beaten by Murless's new stable jockey, George Moore, on Royal Palace, but rides Ribocco to victory in St Leger and Irish Derby. Fifth title with tally of 117.

1968: Wins 2,000 Guineas, Derby, Champion Stakes and Washington International on Sir Ivor. Takes Irish Derby on Ribero, beating Sir Ivor, ridden by Liam Ward, into second place and also rides Ribero to win St Leger. Sixth championship win with 139 successes.

1969: Seventh title with 163 wins. Wins King George VI and Queen Elizabeth Stakes on Park Top and Eclipse Stakes on Wolver Hollow, beating Park Top into second place. Takes first Italian Derby on Bonconte di Montefeltro.

1970: Wins 2,000 Guineas, Derby and St Leger on Nijinsky, first horse to win Triple Crown since Bahram thirty-five years previously. Beaten into second place on Nijinsky in Prix de l'Arc de Triomphe and Champion Stakes. Wins first 1,000 Guineas on Humble Duty. Eighth jockeys' title with 162 wins.

1971: Wins St Leger on Athens Wood. Ninth championship with 162 victories.

1972: Wins fifth Derby on Roberto after owner John Galbreath controversially substitutes him at eleventh hour for Bill Williamson. Gains first success in French Derby on Hard To Beat. Wins seventh St Leger on Boucher. Fourth in table with total of 103.

1973: Gains first success in Prix de l'Arc de Triomphe on Rheingold at seventeenth attempt. Second in table to Willie Carson with 129 wins.

1974: Takes King George VI and Queen Elizabeth Stakes on Dahlia. Again second to Carson in championship with 143 wins.

1975: Wins Oaks and Irish Oaks on Juliette Marny. Rides eight winners at Royal Ascot for the second time, including first of three successive Ascot Gold Cups on Sagaro. Third in table with 113. Awarded OBE.

1976: Wins record seventh Derby on Empery, beating previous record of six held by Jem Robinson and Steve Donoghue. Seventh in table with eighty-seven successes.

1977: First season as contract rider for Robert Sangster. Partners Sangster's colt, The Minstrel, to win the Derby, Irish Derby and King George VI and Queen Elizabeth Stakes and the owner's Alleged to win Prix de l'Arc de Triomphe. Wins Eclipse Stakes on Artaius. Lucky to escape serious injury when his foot is caught in stirrup and he is dragged along by Durtal before the Oaks. Fourth in table with 103 wins.

1978: Rides Alleged to second success in Prix de l'Arc de

Triomphe. Takes Irish 2,000 Guineas, St James's Palace Stakes and Sussex Stakes on Sangster's Jaazeiro. Fifth in championship with ninety-seven victories.

1979: Wins Irish 1,000 Guineas on Sangster's Godetia and Ascot Gold Cup on Le Moss. Sixth in table with seventy-seven wins.

1980: Splits with Sangster, who signs up Pat Eddery for the following season. Wins French Oaks on Mrs Penny. Finishes second to Carson in championship with 156 wins.

1981: First season as contract rider for Henry Cecil. Wins 1,000 Guineas on Fairy Footsteps one week after having ear almost severed in horrific accident in starting stalls at Epsom. Takes over from Walter Swinburn senior to win Oaks on Blue Wind and wins Irish Derby on Shergar in place of suspended Walter Swinburn junior. Lifts tenth title with 179 successes.

1982: Eleventh championship triumph with total of 188. Wins second successive Ascot Gold Cup (eleventh in all) on Ardross, but is beaten into second place on the same horse in the Prix de l'Arc de Triomphe.

1983: Wins ninth Derby on Teenoso. Second in table with 150 winners. Owner Daniel Wildenstein says Piggott will never ride for him again after he partners Awaasif and not Wildenstein's filly, All Along, in Prix de l'Arc de Triomphe. All Along wins the Arc with Walter Swinburn in the saddle, while Awaasif is unplaced.

1984: Gains twenty-seventh British Classic success on Circus Plume in the Oaks, equalling the record set by Frank Buckle 157 years previously. Breaks Buckle's record when winning eighth St Leger on Commanche Run after controversially replacing the colt's regular rider, Darrel McHargue. Wins record seventh King George VI and Queen Elizabeth Stakes on Teenoso. Third in championship with 100 winners, his twenty-fifth century which is an all-time record. Cecil announces he will not be renewing Piggott's contract and signs up Steve Cauthen as stable jockey for the following year.

1985: Peter O'Sullevan breaks news that Piggott is to retire at the end of the season. Gains twenty-ninth Classic success on Shadeed in 2,000 Guineas, but wins only thirty-four races in all as a freelance. Gains last domestic success on Full Choke at Nottingham to bring total of British wins to 4,349. Finishes second on last ride, Wind From The West, on same day.

1986: Begins training at Eve Lodge Stables in Newmarket.

Saddles thirty winners, including a Royal Ascot success with Cutting Blade.

1987: First Classic win as a trainer with Lady Bentley in Italian Oaks. Sentenced to three years' imprisonment for tax evasion on 23 October.

1988: Stripped of OBE. Released from Highpoint Prison on 24 October.

1989: Returns to race riding for first time since retirement when he has three mounts at Monterrico race track in Lima, Peru.

1990: Takes out professional jockey's licence again on 11 October. Four days later finishes close second on first ride back in England aboard Sumonda at Leicester. The following day gains first win on Nicholas, trained by his wife, at Chepstow. Ten days later wins $1 million Breeders' Cup Mile on Royal Academy, owned by Sangster and trained by O'Brien, at Belmont Park, New York.

1991: Finishes seventh aboard Hokusai in first Derby ride since comeback. Rides forty-eight domestic winners.

1992: Takes British Classic tally to thirty when winning 2,000 Guineas for fifth time on Sangster's Rodrigo de Triano. Rides Rodrigo to victory in Irish 2,000 Guineas, York International Stakes and Champion Stakes. Suffers horrific fall aboard Mr Brooks in Breeders' Cup.

1993: Narrowly beaten in 1,000 Guineas on Niche. Adds to amazing record at Royal Ascot with victory on College Chapel, trained by Vincent O'Brien. Father, Keith Piggott, dies aged eighty-nine.

STATISTICS

LESTER PIGGOTT'S EPSOM DERBY RIDES

Year	Mount	Finishing position
1951	Zucchero (28–1) (left at start)	Unplaced
1952	Gay Time (25–1)	2nd
1953	Prince Charlemagne (66–1)	Unplaced
1954	Never Say Die (33–1)	**1st**
1955	Windsor Sun (33–1)	Unplaced
1956	Affiliation Order (33–1)	Unplaced
1957	Crepello (6–4 fav)	**1st**
1958	Boccaccio (20–1)	Unplaced
1959	Carnoustie (10–1)	Unplaced (6th)
1960	St Paddy (7–1)	**1st**
1961	No mount (stayed at home)	
1962	No mount (suspended)	
1963	Corpora (100–8)	Unplaced (5th)
1964	Sweet Moss (100–8)	Unplaced (10th)
1965	Meadow Court (10–1)	2nd
1966	Right Noble (9–2 jt fav)	Unplaced (9th)
1967	Ribocco (22–1)	2nd
1968	Sir Ivor (4–5 fav)	**1st**
1969	Ribofilio (7–2 fav)	Unplaced (5th)
1970	Nijinsky (11–8 fav)	**1st**
1971	The Parson (16–1)	Unplaced (6th)
1972	Roberto (3–1 fav)	**1st**
1973	Cavo Doro (12–1)	2nd
1974	Arthurian (28–1)	Unplaced (12th)
1975	Bruni (16–1)	Unplaced (14th)
1976	Empery (10–1)	**1st**
1977	The Minstrel (5–1)	**1st**
1978	Inkerman (4–1 fav)	Unplaced (21st)

1979	Milford (15–2)	Unplaced (10th)
1980	Monteverdi (8–1)	Unplaced (14th)
1981	Shotgun (7–1)	4th
1982	No mount (intended mount Simply Great injured)	
1983	Teenoso (9–2 fav)	**1st**
1984	Alphabatim (11–2)	Unplaced (5th)
1985	Theatrical (10–1)	Unplaced (7th)
1991	Hokusai (25–1)	Unplaced (7th)
1992	Rodrigo de Triano (13–2)	Unplaced (9th)
1993	Fatherland (8–1)	Unplaced (9th)

35 RIDES   9 WINNERS   4 RUNNERS-UP

LESTER PIGGOTT'S DOMESTIC CLASSIC WINS

Mount	Year	Classic	Prize money (£)
Never Say Die	1954	Derby	16,960
Crepello	1957	2,000 Guineas	13,598
Crepello	1957	Derby	18,660
Carrozza	1957	Oaks	16,101
Petite Etoile	1959	Oaks	21,155
St Paddy	1960	Derby	33,052
St Paddy	1960	St Leger	30,379
Aurelius	1961	St Leger	29,818
Valoris	1966	Oaks	35,711
Ribocco	1967	St Leger	42,696
Sir Ivor	1968	2,000 Guineas	22,587
Sir Ivor	1968	Derby	58,525
Ribero	1968	St Leger	33,437
Nijinsky	1970	2,000 Guineas	28,295
Humble Duty	1970	1,000 Guineas	21,015
Nijinsky	1970	Derby	62,311
Nijinsky	1970	St Leger	37,082
Athens Wood	1971	St Leger	35,743
Roberto	1972	Derby	63,736
Boucher	1972	St Leger	35,709
Juliette Marny	1975	Oaks	44,958
Empery	1976	Derby	111,825
The Minstrel	1977	Derby	107,530
Fairy Footsteps	1981	1,000 Guineas	52,180
Blue Wind	1981	Oaks	74,568

Teenoso	1983	Derby	165,080
Circus Plume	1984	Oaks	122,040
Commanche Run	1984	St Leger	110,700
Shadeed	1985	2,000 Guineas	94,689
Rodrigo de Triano	1992	2,000 Guineas	113,736

TOTAL PRIZE MONEY £1,653,876

162 Classic rides: 35 Derby   36 2,000 Guineas   33 1,000 Guineas
30 Oaks   28 St Leger (up to and including 1993 Derby)

LESTER PIGGOTT'S IRISH WINNERS

Year	No. of winners	
1958	2	(First winner, Rise Above at Phoenix Park 9 August)
1959	1	(Won on Gladness at Phoenix Park 11 August)
1960	0	
1961	0	(First ride in Irish Derby (3rd) and Oaks (2nd))
1962	0	
1963	1	
1964	1	
1965	9	(3 hat-tricks; first Classic win, on Meadow Court in Irish Derby)
1966	1	
1967	8	(Won Irish Derby on Ribocco and St Leger on Dan Kano)
1968	2	(Won Irish Derby on Ribero)
1969	1	
1970	3	(Won Irish 2,000 Guineas on Decies and Oaks on Santa Tina)
1971	11	(4 winners from 4 rides at Leopardstown 2 August; won Irish 1,000 Guineas on Favoletta)
1972	1	
1973	27	(3 hat-tricks)
1974	10	(1 hat-trick)
1975	21	(5 winners from 5 rides at the Curragh 6 September; 3 hat-tricks; won Irish Oaks on Juliette Marny and St Leger on Caucasus)
1976	19	(Won Irish St Leger on Meneval)
1977	9	(Won Irish Derby on The Minstrel)
1978	22	(Won Irish 2,000 Guineas on Jaazeiro)

9	13	(Won Irish 1,000 Guineas and Oaks on Godetia)
1980	6	
1981	1	(Won Irish Derby on Shergar)
1982	0	
1983	1	
1984	0	
1985	6	
1990	6	(4 winners from 5 rides at the Curragh 23 October)
1991	21	
1992	8	(Won Irish 2,000 Guineas on Rodrigo de Triano)
1993	1	

TOTAL IRISH WINNERS 212 (up to 22 May 1993)

LESTER PIGGOTT'S FLAT RACE WINS

Overseas winners

Argentina	2
Australia	19
Bahrein	2
Belgium	4
Brazil	1
Canada	1
Denmark	2
Dubai	3
France	358
Germany	34
Greece	11
Hong Kong	33
India	8
Ireland	212
Italy	37
Jamaica	11
Jersey	2
Kenya	1
Malaysia	30
New Zealand	7
Norway	7
Rhodesia	3
Singapore	45
South Africa	19
Spain	5

Sweden	8
Trinidad	1
USA	13
TOTAL	879

British winners

TOTAL	4,450

(up to and including 1993 Derby)

Statistics compiled by Neal R. Wilkins

PICTURE CREDITS

All-Sport: 157
Associated Press: 171
Ed Byrne: 178
Cambridge Newspapers Ltd: 134
Gerry Cranham: 12, 30, 34, 54, 71, 72, 76 (bottom), 81, 92 (bottom), 98 (bottom), 100, 101, 107, 127 (bottom), 132, 137, 158, 177, 181
David Hastings: 25, 89 (bottom), 139, 159
Hulton-Deutsch Collection: 17, 21, 23 (bottom), 39, 41, 49, 69
Alan Johnson: 110 (right), 118
Trevor Jones: 95, 142, 155, 168, 170
Popperfoto: 15, 23 (top), 26, 28, 43, 45, 47, 51, 56, 76 (top), 79, 92 (top)
Sport & General: 63, 88
Sporting Pictures (UK) Ltd: 105, 110 (left)
Syndication International: 19, 89 (top), 98 (top), 126, 127 (top), 172